Yugoslav Economic Development and Political Change

Richard P. Farkas

The Praeger Special Studies program—utilizing the most modern and efficient book production techniques and a selective worldwide distribution network—makes available to the academic, government, and business communities significant, timely research in U.S. and international economic, social, and political development.

Yugoslav Economic Development and Political Change

The Relationship between Economic Managers and Policy-Making Elites

Praeger Publishers   New York   Washington   London

PRAEGER SPECIAL STUDIES IN INTERNATIONAL ECONOMICS AND DEVELOPMENT

Library of Congress Cataloging in Publication Data

Farkas, Richard P
    Yugoslav economic development and political change.

    (Praeger special studies in international economics
and development)
    Bibliography: p.
    Includes index.
    1. Yugoslavia—Economic policy—1945-   2. Yugoslavia—
Politics and government—1945-   I. Title.
HC407.Y6F26   330.9'497'02   73-13347
ISBN 0-275-28780-7

330.9497
F 229y

PRAEGER PUBLISHERS
111 Fourth Avenue, New York, N.Y. 10003, U.S.A.
5, Cromwell Place, London SW7 2JL, England

Published in the United States of America in 1975
by Praeger Publishers, Inc.

75-2850

© 1975 by Praeger Publishers, Inc.

Printed in the United States of America

Of course, there are many forms and combinations in human groupings through which the evolution process can find its way. However, it seems that the industrial enterprise is a grouping that contains a lot of elements that make it especially apt for a fast growth, particularly in the developed countries. It is usually not hampered by national, political, religious or ideological restrictions, or by a small maximum size (such as the family is).

The balanced and conscious international development of the industrial enterprises is of so much importance because of the sharp acceleration . . . at present taking place in the technological and material sense. Social evolution has to keep up with it . . . . The industrial enterprise being the most important economical motor in the development of the optimal standard of living, one of the essential parameters in the present world, it is of utmost importance on the one hand that its development is not restricted by unnatural measures, on the other hand that it realizes the responsibility it has towards society, not only with regard to the company's employees, not only towards a particular region or nation, but in the long run the responsibility of being one of the carriers of evolution that might influence the eventual fate of the world.

I think that this evaluation of the role of the industrial enterprise becomes more and more obvious and that more and more responsible managers are aware of it. This is quite different from the unqualified search for power and profit that is sometimes attributed to the management of companies as being their sole and only goal.

A. Stikker
(Brockmeyer, M. J. [ed.],
Yugoslav Workers' Self-Management)

It is typical to preface a study with a glowing philosophical thought or quip drawn from the likes of Shakespeare, Marx, or Plato. While tidy, such a thought seems somehow inappropriate to a study as groping and preliminary as this. The above passage has many refutable components and is only in an awkward way elegant. Yet it

captures some of the normative texture of the premises which spurred
the research on which this manuscript is based. Social organization
and social systems are "elegantly awkward" creations of man. And
while man's values can accommodate the heterogeneity and individ-
uality of men, they seem stubbornly reluctant to accept the diversity
of systems devised by men. Families, governments, and a full range
of other types of social organization can be used to illustrate the
point. However, the focus in this study is the relatively modern
universal, the economic enterprise, industrial and agricultural
firms whose social purpose, organization, pattern of behavior, and
leadership may tell us more about ourselves and our "civilizations."

ACKNOWLEDGMENTS

The Department of Government and International Studies at the University of South Carolina, the H. B. Earhart Foundation of Ann Arbor, Michigan, and the Research Foundation of the State University of New York have provided support for this research project. Though by naming a few the danger of omission is great, I would like to offer particular thanks to Professors James A. Kuhlman and Paul W. Blackstock for their incisive criticisms and patient testing of ideas. Their friendship and continuing scholarly challenges are a lasting by-product of our relationship. Professors R. Barry Farrell and Edward Janosik have also contributed greatly; the former by the impetus and challenge imbued some years ago at Northwestern University, and the latter, former Chairman of the Department of Political Science at the State University of New York at Geneseo, by his encouragement and spur to excel.

Mrs. Nancy Steen, Mrs. Patricia James, Mrs. Luella Schumaker, Mr. Bob Madill and Mr. Brian Lynch have contributed secretarial and administrative assistance and for this I offer my appreciation.

The associates, friends, and interviewees in Yugoslavia are owed a most sincere debt of gratitude for their roles in the planning and success of the four field research experiences from 1968 to 1972. I am especially appreciative of the gracious hospitality afforded me by Professor Leo Mates, former Director of the Institute of International Politics and Economics, and Ivan Spika, Director of Industrijsko-Poljoprivredni Kombinat. Many other Yugoslavs—village, trade union, and enterprise leaders; republic and national officials; and members of the international elite—took time from their busy professional schedules to aid in the identification of major developments and changes in the system and to offer solutions and assessments from their varying perspectives.

Finally, I wish to recognize and honor the stalwart support of my wife, Joan, and of my parents whose resilience is an enduring model for me.

CONTENTS

LIST OF TABLES AND FIGURES

Yugoslav Economic Development and Political Change

CHAPTER

1

SYSTEM DESIGN

This research is designed to illuminate the interactions between the politics and the economics of a modern socialist country. Its approaches will emphasize the political significance and implications of decisions made by primarily economic elites at various levels and the systematic policy responses they engender. Depicted in another way, an attempt is made here to analyze a particular and powerful interest group as it penetrates, pressures, and alters the Yugoslav political system. The study will also examine the application of political decisions downward through the system. In this way the full network of channels for political communication to and from the enterprise elite can be reflected in the analysis. The framework then of this analysis is the domestic political and economic system of contemporary Yugoslavia. However, a thorough examination of this subject will not and could not avoid the crucial phases of issues of international economics and politics as they enter and exit the Yugoslav experience.

The motivating interest in this focus for research is a product of a three-pronged disappointment with the store of research and reflection on the most recent stage of development in the states ruled by Communist Parties. These presently fallow areas are nonetheless fertile. The challenge of sowing these concepts is relatively manageable, but the harvest is another matter. This research and its hypotheses as tested represent an initial response to the needs, little more. One might perceive the "gaps" in the literature as follows. First, few political scientists have set about the task of analyzing the role played in socialist states by business elites and economic organization (especially microlevel) in the domestic and foreign politics of states.[1] Business (or whatever the appropriate societal term for management and marketing of goods and services) is both related formally to the government and more crucially, but less obviously, intertwined with

1

the whole political system. Analysts would not deny that business is in politics, or that politics is in business, but few have addressed themselves in a comparative and rigorous way to answering just how these realms are related. One of the intrinsic challenges in this formulation is to provide a working definition for a relatively uncomfortable term (in a noncapitalist system), "business," and to introduce a measure of precision to our description of the observed patterns of economic and political behavior.

A growing portion of the social science literature employs the term "industrial relations" to identify the triadic pattern of government, management, and labor interaction in a system. Research into the dynamic relationship between patterns of industrial relations and political change has stimulated considerable official and scholarly interest, especially in the industrial centers of Europe. In this vein, the comparative significance of this limited study may find reinforcement in the words of B. C. Roberts, President of the International Industrial Relations Association, in his Presidential Address to the Third World Congress in September 1973.

> The international dimension of industrial relations can
> be analysed in terms of changes in the political, eco-
> nomic and social environment. Industrial relations sys-
> tems are bounded by the political entity within which they
> exist. When the political structure is altered, new in-
> fluences have an effect on the pattern of industrial rela-
> tions. The great political changes which have occurred
> in this century have already profoundly altered pre-
> viously established systems of industrial relations. The
> industrial relations systems of the USSR and Eastern
> Europe, for example, are very different from what they
> would have been like had history taken a different
> course. . . . Many of the most important innovations
> in the field of industrial relations have been developed
> in one country and transferred to another. . . . I will
> state simply that I see no reason why this process of
> borrowing political and social ideas should not continue.[2]

Conventional investigations by colleagues in the industrialized societies often prove the manner and extent of the exportation of "Western," which is to say capitalist, forms of economic behavior or practice to contemporary Communist systems. Roberts is sensitized to our importation of ideas from the East European Communist states.

> The revision of European company law so as to bring
> about a greater degree of employee participation in the

2

process of corporate management reflects social trends which are world wide. If I may be permitted to refer to my first Presidential address six years ago, I then suggested that increased worker participation at the plant and company level might well be the pattern towards which industrial relations systems were moving in both Eastern and Western countries. Today, the current support for increased participation is running powerfully in all the advanced industrial countries. . . . Alternative forms of taxation have to be found, which both raise revenue and are anti-inflationary. Ironically, it could be that developments in the centralized economic systems of Eastern Europe, in which collective bargaining plays a less significant role as a mechanism of income determination than in the Western countries, could provide some guidance.[3]

This is merely to point in the direction of changes which are evident to the economic observer. Adaptations of socialist patterns institutionalized in the East European Communist states may be recognized in Holland, West Germany, and Sweden not to mention most serious consideration now being given to some proposals in France, Britain, and Italy. Even the United States corporate elite are showing tangible signs of embracing concepts of participatory economic organization (managerial and worker based) though in significantly qualified forms.

The more focused concern for this research is the comparative significance of the linkage between political change and industrial relations patterns in the East European Communist community. The literature, bolstered significantly by the Gitelman monograph on the diffusion of experimentation and change in the East European region, has now opened the subject of the cross-fertilization of ideas and policies in the area.[4] For our research to be of value it is necessary that the range of national differences and a modest heterogeneity of interests among the East European states be acknowledged. These differences cause variations in capability and motivation which ultimately are reflected in nuances of interstate and domestic strategy. The Yugoslav post-war experience of some three decades must be viewed, in the context of East European politics, as a basic and integral social experiment—a tinkering with a model which has direct and immediate relevance for all other East European states.

For the West, the achievements of Yugoslavia will, for the foreseeable future, highlight one of many alternatives which gain attention and, in some cases, credence when deficiencies in our own system become evident. For the East Europeans the success or failure of the Yugoslav experiment is markedly more critical, their disclaimers notwithstanding. It is not the rise or fall of an alien system but that of a fraternal twin. When congenital weaknesses become evident, all must be alarmed because of the common percentage. When spurts of growth are evident, the sibling rivalry is not easily rationalized away.

As in all examinations of the metamorphic state system in Yugoslavia, and indeed in many of the Communist systems now taking more mature shapes, this investigation represents a theoretical fragment—the substantive and conceptual examination of a principal component in the social system.[5] As such it has only very limited utility as an indicator or, more ambitiously, as a predictor of systemic development. Yet its aim is just that: to reflect on the direction, pace, and impact of accomplished change and to project future developments and their ramifications in systems where some critical variables can be suggested and examined. The identification of such "critical" variables is itself a major undertaking, and in that search this project may have its place.

In part as a result of the trend to discard "political economy" as a framework for academic study, the economic and political sectors of a society are often viewed as independent parts of the whole. In the sense that they can proceed along two different or even contradictory paths, their independent status is certainly evident. In fact, in many developing states (a category into which, according to some criteria, most if not all socialist states could be placed) the paths of the economy and the polity seem to be nonparallel and, in a few contemporary cases, are developing in opposite directions. Illustrations will be found in subsequent chapters. This having been said, however, one could make a case that the very special relationship and interaction between economics and politics must be a subject of more than casual inquiry given that the communist societal design congenitally fuses them.[6] An assumption common in the social sciences is that either the Western democratic or the totalitarian pattern (model) of separation of the "economic" and the "political" is appropriate for the rigorous examination of modern socialist states. Many Western analysts either implicitly or explicitly make and proceed on this assumption. Our need then is for a careful, objective look at the nature of this relationship, both in theory and in practice, in order to provide a more firm foundation on which specific investigation of socialist systems can be built. Colleagues have initiated this endeavor and this research is proposed as a contribution thereto.[7]

Finally, although linked intrinsically to the above, leading scholars are just beginning to pursue the idea of pluralism in socialist political systems, a controversial proposition among some contemporary writers. However, it appears abundantly clear on the basis of field research and recent systemic developments that a degree of pluralism does exist and that, this being the case, pluralism is a valuable and relevant variable for comparative political analysis. Interest groups do exist in Yugoslavia both on a formal and informal, anomic basis. Further, these interest groups have found it possible to expose and articulate their positions within a broad range of issues. One such group, or more accurately, conglomerate of groups, is to be found naturally enough in the economic sector of the society. This project, then, attempts to augment and solidify the case for such analytic approaches made in a few recent publications.[8] These are the perceived shortcomings and challenges of the current state of investigation to which this effort is an initial response.

The comparative literature on socialist and communist systems is limited in quantity, theoretical and methodological consistency, and scope. There exists an imbalance which for classically obvious reasons is weighted on analysis of the Soviet Union and which is not bent in the direction of comparative frameworks. The Yugoslav system has emerged as a focus through an embryonic but impressive flurry of economic research (largely descriptive) which serves this project quite adequately as a base.[9]

The interaction between two major sectors of the societal pattern of any modern state should be of keen interest to the comparative scholar. That such intercourse is real and important is a truism. Yet academia has struggled with a variety of propositions relating to the magnitude, importance, and pattern of these sub-systemic relationships. With the doctrine and program of a socialist philosophy overlaid upon this intriguing debate, the Yugoslav case becomes a focus and indeed a challenge to the social philosopher, the political scientists, the economist, the sociologist, and the management scientist, on the one hand, and the practicing politician, the manager, and the entrepreneur, on the other. An attempt was made to explore and exploit all of these sources in the preparation of this study with the goal of developing a perspective and an academic assessment which transcends the useful but confining parameters of any single discipline.

A conscious and concerted commitment is therefore made to deal with the language, methodological techniques, and conceptualizations of the social sciences to the extent that this researcher is able while minimizing, whereever possible, theoretical complexity and jargon. Strength can be found in the logic and breadth of the social philosopher; in the "science" and methodological innovation of the political scientist, economist, and sociologist; and in the applied expertise of the management scientist. Further, this research would not be complete and would not have been presented had it not been possible to temper all such theory and reflection with the special and exclusive "real world" lens of the practitioner—be he politician, businessman, citizen, or worker.

Before discussion of the research findings, a brief description of the organization of the Yugoslav political and economic subsystems is needed. This is neither a thorough nor rigorously balanced representation of how government in Yugolsavia operates. It is simply an effort to isolate some of the most interesting and provocative elements of that system which appear relevant to the subject of this particular investigation. The following is essentially a structural portrayal which leans heavily on Yugoslav sources for its detail. While this may be criticized as presenting no more than the designs of the system, these seem useful because they do cast light upon the formal structure of society and silhouette a more subjective impression of the tone or complexion of the system. To answer the challenge that some of the propositions (taken from Yugoslav sources) do not accurately reflect the nature of the political process in the state, the following justification is submitted. Yugoslav accounts of their societal organization (a) accurately reflect a concern for and the existence of many channels which link managers with government and the economic interests with the political decision makers; (b) represent an institutionalized approach with an accompanying doctrine which, with the weight of recent changes in Yugoslavia, might be the backbone and design of the post-Tito state; (c) says something about the way Yugoslavs expect the system to operate over time, given that the doctrine and its concomitant organizational forms appear to be popularly supported; (d) provide a point from which the research can speak to the question of how and in which respects the implementation of the system has approached or deviated from the design. A corollary to these points is that the literature and resources on this area are not so well developed that a complete or balanced analysis is available from nonYugoslav sources.

Thus the first task of the investigator is to examine the societal framework in which he will be testing hypotheses and, if possible, to gauge the political and economic environments into which his variables must be fit.

THE CONTEMPORARY DESIGN OF THE
ECONOMIC SYSTEM

Post-war Yugoslavia has passed through several phases of socio-economic and political transformation. From World War II to 1950 all basic means of production were nationalized on the Stalinist model. After 1950 a reassessment of the centralized administrative management of the economy was initiated. This process resulted in

a gradual abandonment of the rigidly hierarchical structure in favor
of a new economic system built upon "worker management" and
functional decentralization. As an official source elaborates:

> Viewed from the economic aspect, social ownership makes
> it possible to shape production according to the needs of
> the community, preventing, at the same time, the aliena-
> tion of the surplus product of the producer, since this
> concept of ownership enables him to decide on the pur-
> pose and distribution of the social product and to acquire
> directly his share of it.[10]

Yugoslavia claims to be the first country in the world to have "turned
the factories over to the workers" for management. They date this
watershed June 1950, and never ignore its implications for all other
(and paternal) socialist countries. In theory no single body or person
is the owner or ruler of socially-owned property, nor are they entitled
to dispose of it at their own discretion or to appropriate the surplus
product obtained from labor with socially-owned means of production.
Private property does exist in the larger part of the agricultural
sector, and to a lesser extent in the handicraft trades. With respect
to private property the official position of the League of Communists
is that the private ownership of various consumer goods and commodities is the citizens' fundamental right and an incentive for individual initiative. The conceptualization of "socialist property" is
a critical one in the matrix of economic theory in Yugoslavia and as
such has received a substantial measure of academic inquiry.[11]
   Production in Yugoslavia has the characteristics of "cash-
commodity production." This simply means that commodities are
produced for the market and are exchanged on the market. Since 1950
when the system of social development plans was introduced, in general
only the basic proportions of production and the distribution of earnings in the socially-owned sector have been determined by plans,
leaving room for initiative on the part of economic organizations.
Initiative, given that the doctrinaire Soviet interpretation of Marxian
initiative has been rejected in thought and practice, remains one of
the much debated "unknowns" of Yugoslav systemic development.
The general relevance of this variable to our study is implied throughout, and dealt with explicitly in Chapters 2 and 3. It may be hypothesized that it is one of those factors or issues which, in a broad sense,
forge the complex link between economics and politics in the system.
   The basic organizational unit of production and economic activity
is the working organization or enterprise. Apart from these enterprises, there are also other associations of producers; agricultural
cooperatives, business associations, and marketing associations. In

the late 1960s and early 1970s the style, role, and organization of these entities have changed significantly, leading to new dynamic relationships in the system. Such changes are treated as "organizational developments" in Chapter 4. Economic enterprises may be established not only by political or territorial authorities but also by producers themselves. The autonomy of all such enterprises is suggested quite simply by the passage: "The economic enterprise has the status of a legal person and conducts its business independently."12 The economic enterprise is managed by its working collective, either directly or through the bodies elected by the latter. These "representative" bodies are the workers' council and the board of management. After paying federal and other taxes prescribed by law, the enterprises have at their disposal the total income they have earned. Various Federal policies provide incentives for reinvestment of such funds. The enterprise is at liberty to increase its working capital by entering into financing arrangements with banks or it may form associations with other enterprises for the purpose of expanding operations. This integrative form of organizational change is discussed in Chapter 3. The Constitution provides that all of Yugoslavia is a single market and that all enterprises may appear on this market with equal rights.

Two key features of the economic system in the Socialist Federal Republic are: the business associations and the economic chambers. Generally, both of these units coordinate diverse business efforts, nurture business arrangements, and attempt to maximize the rational utilization of capital. The chambers are bodies for economic management, in the broadest sense, at the district, provincial, republic, and Federal levels. The business associations are multi-enterprise arrangements to coordinate some aspect of business policy which enhances the parties (enterprises) relative position in the economy. Basically, they may, among other things, buy, market, and advertise together when it is in their common interest to do so.

The system of worker management in economic organizations is functionally linked to changes in the character of the commune through its noneconomic counterpart, social "self-government." In a formal sense, it is the responsibility of the commune to insure conditions of economic activity and accommodate the broader social needs of the workers within its jurisdiction. The commune passes long-term economic development plans, annual plans, and the budget. It is authorized to establish working organizations (such as factories and shops), earmark funds for the financing of individual branches, monitor the work and activities of all organizations in its area, and supervise the utilization of public resources. Representatives of working organizations and private citizens can participate in discussions at the sessions of the communal assembly if the agenda includes questions of interest to them.

Within this framework the bodies of worker management have a considerable range of flexibility (policy and behavior). Within their scope are decisions on the use of depreciation and investment funds, decisions to expand or contract the scope of business activity, and decisions to introduce new production or technical processes. In principle, the enterprise direktor[13] must interact with the workers' council to arrive at each decision.

THE DESIGN OF THE POLITICAL SYSTEM

Since 1950, the role of the State (governmental) machinery and centralized administrative management has diminished as a result of a series of organizational and policy adjustments. The political units in the Socialist Federal Republic are the communes, districts, republics, and Federation. The Federation consists of six constituent republics—Serbia, Croatia, Slovenia, Bosnia-Hercegovina, Macedonia, and Montenegro.[14] The "cautious" delineation of greater autonomy for the republics has marked Titoist political policy in the early 1970s.[15] Each republic is divided into districts and these into communes. The highest organ of government and "representative of the people's sovereignty" is the Federal Assembly.[16]

With half of its members elected every other year, this assembly is responsible for constitutional changes, legislation, and referenda. It passes on economic plans, determines the guidelines for foreign policy, decides on war and peace and on international treaties and agreements, and formulates all other policy of "broad social importance." A Federal Executive Council is the arm of the Assembly responsible for the implementation of laws and supervision of the Federal administration. This cabinet-like body is also the sponsor of most significant legislation. The Republican Assemblies are limited by the frameworks of the Federal Constitution, the Republic's Constitution, and the Federal laws. Both assemblies, the Federal and the Republican, have five chambers. The district and commune assemblies have just two chambers each, the district or communal council and the council of producers (economic organizations). This organizational delineation and dichotomy of political power at the local level is illuminating. Only if the council of producers is sharply divided will the enterprise direktors forfeit their considerable influence over local policy matters. This structural arrangement is not only consistent with ideological necessities in a socialist state but also provides a viable and substantial political role for the enterprise leadership, and in this way establishes a significant guarantee that local political policy will not fly in the face of the environment necessary for enterprise operation and development. In effect, the enterprises are challenged with the responsibility of a major role in political policy.

9

The five chambers of the Federal Assembly are (a) the Federal Chamber; (b) the Economic Chamber (Savezne Privredni Komore); (c) the Cultural-Educational Chamber; (d) the Chamber of Social Welfare and Public Health; and (e) the Organizational-Political Chamber. Each chamber has 120 deputies who, in the case of the Federal Chamber, are elected directly and, in the other cases, are appointed by the communal assemblies within the guidelines of the Federal chamber whose membership is in question. The chambers discharge the affairs within their spheres of jurisdiction either independently or in conjunction with the other chambers. The Federal Chamber, acting on terms of "equality" with the Economic Chamber, deliberates on matters in the sphere of the economy, passes laws and other acts in this sphere, and lays down the Federal Social Development Plans (annual and long-term). Each chamber is entitled to make recommendations to the appropriate autonomous bodies and state authorities. All such "representative" bodies (chambers) employ various committees and commissions as well as special technical and expert services in preparing policy recommendations.

The chambers are designed to function both formally and informally. They provide formal representation of enterprise interests at the local, republic, and national levels. Though it remains unclear that the pentagonal chamber structure at the Federal level is based upon a realistic projection of how a modern system operates or which interests (groups) want and need direct representation, the organizational design does adroitly anticipate the focused need for the enterprise elite to have access to and a visible role in the national political process. Other political systems, including many highly developed ones, force the interests of the business elite and the corporate structure to be articulated through a complex maze of informal channels. Thus, a key feature of the political life of those systems is removed from public awareness and scrutiny. The Yugoslav system, however, does not fully eliminate the "invisible" political promotion of interests suggested above. Chapter 4 embraces these and other dimensions of linkages between political and economic centers of power in the system.

Among the judicial components of the system, one which is pertinent to the economic and industrial sectors is the Supreme Economic Arbitration Court. The republics also have courts which limit their adjudication to cases and issues of a primarily economic nature. All legal codes and statutes are based on constitutional principles; however, statutes may differ, often significantly, by reflecting specific features of individual communes or republics—particularly the level and type of economic and social development. Consequently, the statute of one commune may formally and functionally give priority to the development of industry, another to tourism, and a third to agriculture. Often reflecting and representing these distinctive features and interests in the system are professional and industrial associations whose form and purpose vary widely.[17]

On the national level, two nongovernmental political organizations hold central positions in the social matrix of the contemporary state. It will be hypothesized that their role is one of those most rapidly changing factors in the juxtaposition of political power in Yugoslavia. The Socialist Alliance of Working People of Yugoslavia (SAWPY), a mass-based political organization, rallies support from the economic sector on the policy proposition that "there can be no socialism without democracy, which is primarily reflected in the right of producers to manage the economy and independently distribute the fruits of their work."[18] This suggests an economic priority in the SAWPY program, but in a more general sense the Alliance works, in its own words, to quell "all forms of administrative or political pressure in relations between the rural and urban population"—a most meaningful formulation in the Yugoslav developmental context. Another interpretation of the SAWPY's national purpose is "to develop their political initiative and activity in the building of socialism and socialist social relations."[19] It has designated to it the role of overseer of elections and the political processes. The Alliance is structured with regular congresses as decision-making forums between which a Central Federal Board directs its political activities. The Federal Board forms specialized commissions to delve into specific policy areas.

The League of Communists in Yugoslavia (LCY) is undoubtedly the most powerful, explicitly political organization, although in increasingly subtle ways. Its organizational structure is not unlike the Socialist Alliance, hierarchical and mass-based,[20] but differs in a few features as a result of a thorough introspection and reorganization which was announced at the Ninth Party Congress in March 1969. The LCY remains one of those networks through which groups can effectively influence policy by articulating interests via the national political elite. The role of the LCY as revealed by interview research is discussed further on in the text of this study.

Both of these organizations serve as means for articulating, influencing, and gauging political developments in the state. Beyond this, both are vehicles for cooptation of political leadership. As such, they seem to have sacrificed a measure of ideological commitment, especially in the case of Sawpy, to establish and maintain a pragmatic political position in the overall political system.

PLANNING AND ECONOMIC DEVELOPMENT

The key instrument of general developmental and economic planning is the Federal Development Plan. From this all-encompassing plan the respective republican plans are sketched. Like the broader plan, these are attempts to balance the development of various regions and economic sectors and to determine the balance of production, consumption, and services appropriate to the area over which they have jurisdiction. Economic enterprises in turn adopt the "independent plans," so-called because they are passed on by each workers' council. To be sure, these enterprise-level plans are well within the guidelines established by the tasks and instruments prescribed by the higher level plans. The format of the plan is now rather classic, although the content is far less patterned. The volume of production, investments, employment, and distribution of income are all projected and/or regulated by the enterprise plan.

Planning is guided by a set of principles, utopian in design, which may illustrate the essential concerns of the planning establishment. These are that development plans should be drawn (a) on the basis of scientific studies and analyses of the development of individual branches of the economy; (b) comprehensively, accounting for all factors in production; (c) universally, giving the communal plans a basic consistency; and (d) only after public discussion, and accepted only after having been passed democratically.

Further, one might well be able to tentatively identify the participants and seats of power in the central Yugoslav policy process by probing the institutional process for plan formulation and acceptance. Upon submission of the first drafts of federal or republic plans, various committees or commissions of the Executive Councils analyze them. They are then referred to the appropriate assembly. Here the plans are examined by the chambers directly concerned with the subject matter of the plans, but in all cases by the economic and general chambers. The Federal Development Plan, for example, is considered and passed on by both the Federal and Economic Chambers of the Federal Assembly. On both the communal and district levels the procedure for passing plans is more involved. The competent councils of local assemblies study the plans. A plan must pass the councils for social planning and finance. The draft plans are then submitted for public discussion to political, social, and professional organizations and to enterprises. The council of planning is then required to review and decide on amendments, publicly justifying their decision if they choose not to amend as recommended by the reviewing groups. The assembly finally adopts the plan and has a responsibility to report its action to all groups. On the question of the initiation of the original first draft of the plan, local officials and others interviewed point (as formal provisions do ambiguously) to "special expert bodies" who bear actual power and responsibility for the direction and bulk of such plans. The Federal Institute of Social Planning and similar (formal and informal) regional and local "brain trusts" are the primary sources of such expertise. Large firms or enterprises also have "analytical planning bureaus or sections" whose membership can be generalized to include the enterprise management elite. None of these planning units are supposed to be controlled by or subordinated to any larger political organization—a provision of more than passing significance to the system, although the application of the principle is incomplete. The economic enterprise itself operates under a plan or series of plans. These commonly cover a period of several years and are often labelled "investment development programs."

REFORMS

June 1965 marked a reformist watershed in the socio-economic development of Socialist Yugoslavia. Of all the reform's formal provisions, three seem of particular and specific concern for the hypotheses under examination in this project.

- The prices of a number of key raw materials were fixed at a higher level, while those of certain other raw materials were allowed to be formed freely;
- The economic enterprises were given the "maximum freedom" in availing themselves of all funds earned in their business transactions authorizing them to utilize such funds to optimize enterprise growth and development; and
- The banking system and its credit policies were more strictly regulated with special regard to international transactions.

The broad design of the "Economic Reform—1965" was to "relieve the Yugoslav market from a non-incentive, custom-tariff policy and expose Yugoslav enterprises to keener international competition."[21] The anticipated ends of this reform are the creation of incentives to raise industrial productivity, stimulation of business activity and economical business methods, and establishment of a "normal" price relationship between raw material producers and manufacturing industries. The thinking, substance, and tone of the system-wide alterations in poignantly indicated. It stands in contrast with the publicly-proclaimed objectives of economic reform in other Communist states. One short-range effect of the program outlined above was to compel some firms and factories to close down due to their inability to survive without protection. The reforms, by insisting on profitable production, have created new conditions for joint transactions of economic enterprises both domestic and foreign, a subject for more focused treatment later. The development of such transactions or associations in conjunction with the activities of the banks in financing and other services is designed to serve as a catalyst to the circulation of capital and the growth of a more vibrant economy.[22] Policy modifications since the introduction of the Reform do not fundamentally alter its direction and meaning. The series of alterations, generally in the vein of creating restraining measures, have been introduced over the nine years following the initial Reform. Since August 1971, anticipated and realized problems of inflation (perceived by the Yugoslavs to be an incumbent cost of rapid systemic change) have drawn the consistent attention of Yugoslav policy-makers.

The politics of the reform movement should be mentioned briefly at this point. Many accounts of the reforms may be found in the literature. One account, representative yet concise, is taken from Deborah Milenkovitch's recent work, Plan and Market in Yugoslav Economic Thought.

> It was the Eighth Congress of the League of Communists, meeting in December, 1964, that resolved the political issue in favor of decentralization and the constitutional principles of the separation of the political and economic spheres. It was still another year before the opponents of reform were purged from the party and the whole-hearted commitment to implementing the reforms was made.[23]

She dates the full and irrevocable reformist victory with the political demise of Aleksandar Rankovic in July 1966 at the Brioni meetings. He is characterized as the "leading political opponent of liberalization."[24]

In a technical sense, the first thrust of change (1950-54) disengaged the central authorities' control over production decisions; the second, uncertain from 1961 to 1965, finally usurped the power of the planning bureaucracy to direct investment. However, political conflict molded if not determined the final outcome of the polemic. There were strong indications that the Yugoslav political elite was unable to come to an agreement over the desirable level and quality of planning, causing an "unacceptable" level of political instability over the issue and subsequently throughout the echelons of the system.[25] Thus, the critical decisions were made and the unsightly but inevitable political casualties removed. More recently, similar tolls have been avoided by virtue of the fact that discussions and criticisms of economic development, and even of the politics of economic decisions, are no longer linked with political unreliability. One can note more than ten incidents in 1972-73 alone which generated sharp debate over basic issues but in which all of the principals (enterprise direktors) emerged with their positions (enterprise and political) intact.

The objective of this research should be placed in the general context of the compelling need to understand the relationship, congenitally and dynamically, between the nature of the industrial sector of a society and the political process and organization in that society. The Yugoslav case provides one clear opportunity for observing particular types of change in both arenas which in turn generate hypotheses which may be valid across Communist systems and, indeed, in other industrial and political systems.

SUMMARY

A few propositions are unavoidable given the design of the contemporary Yugoslav system. The first is that industrial enterprises and firms are very centrally located in the scheme of the Yugoslav state. It is equally clear that whether for popularity and support, for theoretical reasons, or for efficiency, the system is designed to facilitate the penetration and articulation of a large measure of economic interests. Second, one can identify a trend toward greater latitude for entrepreneurial maneuvering within both the economy and the polity. Finally, the tangible significance of an international dimension of the developments in Yugoslavia can be discerned. Both Yugoslav policy to establish a high exposure outside the system and a sanctioned acceptance of external models and routines (especially in business and technology) have marked a search by the Yugoslavs for systemic development which may be unequalled in the Yugoslav state's cosmopolitan heritage or in the development of any contemporary Communist state.[26] In some ways the Yugoslav society of today is both classically socialist and uniquely Yugoslav. Formal, institutional recognition of the role of the managers and the managerial and industrial interest groups is apparent in numerous organizational schemes already discussed. This is a signal not only that the political establishment feels it must, at least in some limited ways, be responsive to the espoused needs of the managerial elite, but that within that elite there exists the expertise which the regime and the society need. In a modern socialist system the primary measure of prestige and success must come from an expanding and vigorous industrial sector over which a distinct elite has at least a guiding role. The Yugoslav polity and its structures do seem to be equipped to be relatively sensitive to each shift, development, and demand from the economy and particularly from the direktors. Direktors collectively emerge as the ball bearing of a newly designed machine which, at this most difficult, initial stage is heating up from inflationary, political, and technological friction.

The problem of analyzing the politics surrounding the decisions and the organizational and functional routines of the economy is, for purposes of this study, divided into three principal sections: the "microlevel" (Direktors, Enterprises, and Politics), linkages (interests of the Economic Sector and Policy-makers), and the "macrolevel" (National Economic Programs and Political Capability; Foreign Economic Policy and the Eastern European Subsystem). In each chapter some effort is made to identify the political issues, to examine the resultant tensions, and to analyze their significance for the Yugoslav system as a whole.

NOTES

1. The International Studies of Values in Politics research leading to Values and the Active Community, Free Press, New York, 1971, may be the only study to confront these elites within their broad social and political environments.

2. B. C. Roberts, "Presidential Address to the Third World Congress on Industrial Relations," Monograph of the International Industrial Relations Association, September, 1973, London School of Economics and Political Science, London, England, p. 12.

3. Ibid., p. 16.

4. Zvi Gitelman, The Diffusion of Political Innovation: From Eastern Europe to the Soviet Union, Sage Professional Paper, Beverly Hills, 1971.

5. The criteria for a comprehensive and cogent "theory" would include a set of explanations of the phenomena observed in this research. While this study does move beyond the purely descriptive by offering limited typologies and partially solidified predicitve models, the level of confidence to be found in this study's power of explanation is clearly modest. Beyond that the focus is on but one of the active sectors of the social system and, as such, the conclusions must be tested by empirical analysis of other social groups within Yugoslavia and components of other socialist systems.

6. The primacy of industrialization as a societal goal, the deposition of political authority and citizenship as a function of participation in productive activity (labor), and the compulsive bond between the political and economic fortunes of the system stand as but a few of the tenets of modern Marxist-Leninist doctrine which mechanistically fuse the polity and the economy. This proposition is tenable in spite of the constitutional principle established at the Eighth LCY Congress prescribing the separation of the political and economic spheres. A further discussion of this phenomenon may be found in Rudolf Bicanic, "Economics of Socialism in a Developed Country," Foreign Affairs, Vol. 44, No. 4, July 1966, pp. 633-50.

7. The following were selected on the basis of recently presented or published scholarly research on the subject: Ichak Adizes, Milovan Djilas, Deborah Milenkovich, Egon Neuberger, Svetozar Pejovich, Karl-Ernst Schenk, Harry Shaffer, Rudi Supek, William Welsh, and Peter Wiles. It is of some significance that only one of the scholars above is a political scientist by training.

8. H. G. Skilling and Franklyn Griffiths (eds.), Interest Groups in Soviet Politics, Princeton University Press, Princeton, 1971.

9. See selected bibliography.

10. "Medjunarodna politika," Beograd, Nemanjina 34, E/18, p. 2.

11. D. Milenkovitch, Plan and Market in Yugoslav Economic Thought, Yale University Press, New Haven, 1971.

S. Pejovich, The Market-planned Economy of Yugoslavia, University of Minnesota Press, Minneapolis, 1966.

S. Pejovich, "The Role of Property Rights in Economic Analysis," panel paper presented to the AAASS, March, 1972.

E. Clayton, "Property Rights: Socialist and Capitalist Systems," panel paper presented to the AAASS, March, 1972.

12. "Medjunarodna politika," p. 4.

13. "Direktor" is used throughout this study as the generic term for the principal enterprise administrator/manager (generalni direktor). While all firms generally have such a figure, parallels with other socio-economic systems are imperfect (especially the "director" in the American corporate system). For this reason, the Serbo-Croat term is employed literally for clarity.

14. Two "autonomous regions" are also contained within the Yugoslav state—Vojvodina and Kosovo-Metohija. They were formed "because of the specific conditions which have governed the historical and cultural evolution of the area in question." This ethnic patch-quilt represented by the republics and regions has manifest political meaning in the contemporary state reflected in the bulk of academic research on Yugoslavia.

15. The increase of autonomy via "decentralization" has been measured by calculated impulse in selected areas of social and political policy and by varying official "interest and enthusiasm" at different points in time.

16. O. Lakicevic (ed.), A Handbook of Yugoslavia, Secretariat for Information of the Federal Executive Council, Review Publications, Belgrade (no publication date), pp. 113-114. This is both an interpretive and an official assessment.

17. It follows that most industrial associations have difficulty divorcing themselves from regional or republic "interests."

18. Medjunarodna politika," Beograd, Nemanjina 34, E/10, p. 2. Also "Socialist Alliance of Working People of Yugoslavia," Review of International Affairs, Belgrade, 1965.

19. Ibid.

29. An impressive unpublished study of the Yugoslav Socialist Alliance was conducted by Professor G. Edward Janosik in 1969.

21. "Medjunarodna politika," Beograd, Nemanjina 34, E/23, p. 1.

22. A comprehensive analysis of this point may be found in the report of proceedings of the Eighth Congress of the League of Communist of Yugoslavia, Practice and Theory of Socialist Development in Yugoslavia (original title: Osmi kongres Saveza komunista Jugoslavije - Praksa i Teorija Izgradnije Socijalisma u Jugoslaviji), Medjunarodna Politika, Beograd, 1965, pp. 57-113.

23. Milenkovitch, op. cit., p. 175.

24. Ibid.

25. The conflict was particularly visible in Belgrade and the republic capitals which, coupled with the uncertainty of inflationary economic trends, brought many analysts of the Yugoslav scene to offer a grim prognosis for the reforms.

26. Herein one may find the critical meaning of this research project and other contemporary research efforts on Communist systems. The Yugoslav path offers clear contrasts to other Communist systems while it labors to work within a common (perceived) conceptual framework for society. As the ramifications emerge, the social scientist hastens to gauge the experiment with due caution, as it shapes our world but cognizant of our challenge to project its meaning for tomorrow's societies.

2

DIREKTORS,
THE ENTERPRISE,
AND POLITICS

In the reformed, decentralized system of the economy, the direktor (top executive management position in the firm) has taken on a crucial series of functions and responsibilities formerly (and doctrinally) far from his professional realm. "Direktor" will be used in this study as the label for the central management figure in the firm. This is done because it is the indigenous term and because the danger exists that some would confuse the Western corporate "director" with the Yugoslav "direktor." The latter is functionally much closer to the role prescribed in the capitalist system as the corporate "president" though the contrasts between these roles will also become evident as this analysis unfolds. In Yugoslavia's socialist system the firm is given the generic title of "enterprise." This seems an appropriate label because under the contemporary policy and program of decentralized decision-making the measure of economic success and the longevity of the firm are very much a function of the direktor's enterprise, that is, initiative. Generally, his is an aggressive role both in a business sense and in a political and organizational context. Simply put, the economic system is currently structured to facilitate and, in fact, solicit assertive and firm decisions by the top management of Yugoslav economic units. The principal restraint on those who might develop "bourgeois" characteristics is the direktor's responsibility to the worker's council. While innumerable research efforts and publications have taken up the subject of the role of the workers' councils under the new system, there appears to be no single treatment in English of the reforms and developments focusing on the role and perspective of the direktor. From this angle, the functional organization appears significantly different from some of the assessments in the current literature.[1]

A very brief biographical portrait of this elite is presented as a foundation from which discussion of the role of this group at various levels of the system may follow. The typical direktor is 47 years old (in 1973) and has held his position in the enterprise for nine and one-half years. He has a degree in economics, is a member of the LCY, and has had some exposure to or experience in one of the "chambers" (usually economic) at the district, republic, or national level.[2] In a very preliminary way, this can suggest to us that (1) the prominent economic elite, as a group, are fully committed to the direction and content, if not to the degree, of reform and decentralized autonomy in the system, and (2) that the typical direktor has some significant degree of awareness of political realities. Such deductions give rise to a general hypothesis that direktors in the Yugoslav socialist system of the 1970s have formidable political "interests" by virtue of their commitments and expectations. This mitigates against their being relegated to the role of "technicians of the economy" (classic in the Soviet model) and emphasizes their "creative" role. A Marxist, cautious of the indictment of "capitalist tendencies" (entrepreneurship), seems able, at least in the Yugoslav context, to reformulate his role in terms of a "vanguard" (leadership) function with goals that are entirely commensurate with socialist property and development. Hence, the rationalization of an untidy theoretical (doctrinaire) challenge to the Yugoslav type of change at the microlevel of economic and political organization.[3]

Most enterprise direktors are cautious about assessments of the practicality of the workers' participation program and about the dynamics which, in an organizational sense, follow from its prescriptions. Probing and lengthy interviews with some prominent economic men in the Socialist Federal Republic lead to certain propositions based on their response.[4]

The change in the role of the workers' councils, so central to the reorganization of the overall Yugoslav system, is an initial focus for this analysis because it has implications of a political as well as of an economic nature, given indications and expectations that decisions of both types will be made on the local level.

Despite the predominantly economic character of the reforms of the 1960s, the view of those in Belgrade is that the decisions made in conjunction with those reforms were based on essentially political criteria.[5] One highly placed interviewee said "it was a political decision, by politicians, on fundamentally political criteria." Of those few who offered an assessment of the power behind the reforms, the most frequently named individual was Edvard Kardelj. Generally, it was implied that he was the member of the leadership responsible for the initiation and impetus behind the changes. This assessment of the political nature of the reforms was bolstered by numerous arguments which reflected skepticism about the ultimate economic applicability, in principle or in practice, of such a sharp reversal

20

in the management relationship in the individual enterprise. As the argument goes, this difficulty would be most acutely appreciated by the economic elite themselves, therefore it is unlikely that they would have pressed for (that is, initiated) such reforms. Two other factors diminish the likelihood that the economic sector as a whole would have initiated the reforms. First, the 1965-67 reforms liberalized importation and thereby competition under which a significant portion of Yugoslav industry could not and did not survive.[6] Second, and more subtle, in answer to questions relating to Party support (at republic and local levels) for the decentralization, an overwhelmingly positive, supportive response was forthcoming with such consistency that one might be led to suggest that only a political decision on political criteria in line with (or in response to) the interests of the subnational Party units could engender that degree of advocacy. This appeared in informal as well as in interview situations.

The political motivation on the part of the national leadership may be reflected in the concerns of a few highly placed political and academic figures interviewed. One often identified political factor was the pressure of the Soviet Union and its systemic hegemony in Eastern Europe, a constant source of political discussion in Yugoslavia and one that was particularly acute after the Czech incident. The Czech crisis illustrated what political pragmatists have understood throughout Eastern Europe for some time. The Yugoslav reforms were politically expedient vis-a-vis bloc relations. They tangibly punctuated Yugoslavia's independent path to socialism and were a bold commitment, if an extremely ambitious one, toward three simultaneous goals: participation, modernization (urbanization), and development (economic).[7] On the subject of "Stalinization," one conservative political figure suggested, "There is a 'passive' resistance to re-Stalinization . . . a latent force [Stalinization] which Yugoslav politics has not yet escaped." Re-Stalinization is commonly conceptualized in Yugoslavia as a return to the Soviet model or matrix of systemic interrelationships. In the year from Spring 1969 to Spring 1970 the "re-Stalinization" of the Soviet system itself was also a prominent subject of discussion throughout Eastern Europe. This external environment is one political dimension of the mixture of causal factors which underlie the reforms.

Domestic politics is another. Pluralism based primarily on nationalism had consistently pressured for policy which would functionally decentralize the system. The Tito leadership circle clearly appreciates the political credibility of such a volatile force reflected in recent adjustments in the system such as the new constitutional amendments and Tito's own proposal for a collegium to accommodate the impending leadership succession. Such impact can be seen in the central theme of the reforms: political participation through decision-making in the enterprise. A very polished, sophisticated banker categorically remarked, "Politicians would not move from this policy [workers' self-management]."

Yet another rationale of a political nature was offered which warrants mention. The argument was impassioned and persuasive while couched in broadly theoretical terms not altogether inconsistent with the Tito leadership. The source was a Croat of high position described by others in the system as "an organizer, a much needed man indispensable to the system." His comment: "The purpose of, the reason for decentralization is to humanize the polity and the economy—to involve man." This is a much echoed theme in Yugoslavia and one which is not without its convincing aspects when mouthed by the economic pragmatists of the system. The case must be qualified by one other very real and important issue. Some of those in the economic sector perceived the advantages and sound economic rationale for the decentralization of power, legitimizing independent industry-wide or even enterprise decisions. This was to be the second of the two principal thrusts of the reforms and with this advantage the direktors and managers could accommodate many other problems.

On the balance sheet, the new relationship between the Direktor and workers' council has not turned out to be a mammoth problem, a "ball and chain," for the typical direktor in Yugoslavia. The workers' councils established early in the systemic development of Socialist Yugoslavia had been invested with the power to participate in the guidance of their working unit. With the reforms of the mid- and late-1960s their explicit role was enhanced in that the system prescribed that worker management (worker self-government) is "obligatory," that it must be "direct management," and that the workers' council and other bodies of worker management "shall be the highest organs of management."[8] Previous to these reforms the constitution had prescribed the role and rights of the management board and the direktor as well as stipulating that the "local social community" (the commune) be involved in the selection of the enterprise direktor. The reforms dissolved these provisions, simultaneously vesting a large measure of autonomy in the enterprises while explicitly elevating the role of the workers' councils. Though the impetus for such changes in the economic system seems to have been political, the rationale is economic (expanding and extending economic capability by nurturing an environment for enterprise development), and an apparently valid one on comparative grounds (conclusions in Chapter 6). Greater latitude to create local goals and incentives to achieve them, and greater flexibility to accommodate "integration and inter-connection through various forms of business cooperation and other types of collaboration," were the two needs of the vast cross section of managers before the reforms.

This new juxtaposition of powers creates for the direktor a
situation which has political and social meaning beyond his need to
realign himself in a management (organizational) sense. Initially,
one might be led to examine Party influence in the enterprise. A
Party unit can be found in every enterprise but it no longer has an
institutionalized role in the determination of policy. It can in fact
play a role, but it is a severely diminished on even in those industries
which are more conservative, either by virtue of their business policy
or of closer centralized control from Belgrade (commodity price
control, and so forth). Examples of such politically "conservative"
sectors are agriculture, the steel industry, and transport. One direktor of a very largé agricultural kombinat (cooperative) explained,
"The Party has a concrete, down to Earth, non-highly-ideological
involvement in life." It is accepted as "natural" that nearly all direktors of major enterprises are members of the LCY, but one can
observe a sharp difference in the propensity of direktors to hold central Party offices between rural and urban areas and along certain
industrial lines.

The urban-rural dichotomy is a difficult one and one that should
not be pressed too far. However, a clear pattern emerges if one ex-
amines the direktors' own reports of his own Party activity either in
terms of offices held or time spent in Party-associated capacities.
Allowing for the subjective quality and problems of validity of the
data generated in interview responses, one is still able to clearly
identify a trend of increased "Party activity" as the size of the community decreases. Rural, agricultural communities reflect, at least
at the level of the local elite, an intense group dynamics which directly
involved enterprise direktors in political, and more specifically,
Party roles. Urban direktors are considerably more detached from
consistent Party activity though they make other adjustments in their
professional schedules and activities to retain a minimum visibility.
The basic correlation suggested here is skewed both by a smaller
population of enterprise direktors at the rural end of the scale, and
by a modest reversal in the trend as it trails off to the extreme rural
end of the scale.

Size of enterprise (regardless of criteria) does not appear to
provide any useful correlations. Type of industry or industrial sector
provides modest guidelines, with those indicated above as "conservative" sectors showing general increases of Party activity. It is difficult to view this apart from the urban-rural variable, however, given
geographic and demographic requisites of various industries.

In some ways most curious is the incidence of Party activity
of the direktors' spouses. Most intense in the range indicated in
Table 1 (by cross-hatching), wives of direktors, especially in towns
and small cities, take an active role and in some cases a proxy-like

23

TABLE 1

Party Activity and Urban/Rural Environments

Question: In terms of offices held and time spent in other LCY* activities, would you assess your involvement as . . .	Urban[a]	Rural[b]	Total
I: "minimal"	9	0	9
II: "very limited"	13	4	17
III: "modest"	14	11	25
IV: "substantial"	9	6	15
V: "primary"	3	5	8
No response or uncodable response	10	14	24
Total	58	40	98

*Including Party activity at local or republic levels.

[a]Urban—enterprises based in Beograd, Zagreb, Sarajevo, Titograd, Skopje, Zadar, Ljubljana, Rijeks, Split.
[b]Rural—all other enterprises.

Note: Scaling—as an alternative to the above dichotomy, the towns and cities were placed on a scale based on size (largest to smallest).

Source: Compiled by the author.

role in Party affairs. It may be noted in general, though on the basis of a very small sample, that wives tend to be highly politicized and astutely aware of local and, in some cases, national political developments.

One recent analysis of the "forces that influence enterprise decisions" suggests a breakdown along these lines.[9]

Internal	External
Working collective	Organs of local government
Workers' council	Organs of federal and republican government

Internal	External
Management board	
Direktor	Confederation of Trade Unions
Factory union organization	Economic chambers and associations
Political party	Political party

This treatment further posits, "the unique feature of the Yugoslav method of decentralization of economic and political organization is that each of these bodies may exert some influence on the decision of the individual firms."[10] The lists above point to the Party as an important factor in the behavior of the firm. One prominent reason (though many could be cited) is that it has a dual linkage—access to both the internal and external environments of the enterprise. This dual capability bears significant political potential, but assessments of the degree to which the Party manipulates or exercises this direct influence are highly controversial. Anthony Sylvester, economic analyst for the Financial Times (London), recently wrote, "many people in the East [East Europe] have chosen to take the concept of management by workers in Yugoslavia too literally, and to ignore the dominant role which the Communist Party continues to play in the country's society and industrial life."[11] Another, apparently more empirically sound evaluation, is taken from Milenkovitch's chapter on Market Socialism. "The purely political influence of the League of Communists cannot be neglected. But the League emphasizes the indirect influence of members as individuals on the enterprises, rather than direct intervention by the part."[12]

These formulations of LCY power and style of affecting enterprise policy spurred examination of this central question in the interviewing of direktors in Yugoslavia. As indicated earlier, the overwhelming conclusion indicated by the interview data comes much closer to Milenkovitch's qualified assessment of Party influence. The nature and history of the Yugoslav Communist system would prevent the utter rejection of Sylvester's caution. However, it must be recognized that a qualitative change, from "control" to "influence" (and indirect at that), indicates a systemic development of major significance at the microlevel of economic and political decision-making. Numerous incidents related to outspoken critics of the new program and the resulting sanctions of the system can be interpreted as indicators of systemic flux.[13]

As stated earlier, the potential problems which would develop through the new emphasis on the worker as decision-maker have been finessed with great skill and concomitant success. As documented earlier, in principle, the workers make policy and directly manage the enterprise. It was also suggested that with a more "open" and competitive economy, direktors need expert advice and executive license to make complex and innovative decisions. The interview data would indicate that those direktors confronted by this apparent dilemma have resolved it in a preliminary and functionally operational way. This involved agreement on a set of management routines and a common set of priorities for their enterprises. One might argue that the resolution of these conflicting demands was indeed predisposed by the nature of the reforms, the economic circumstances, and the tangible and pragmatic needs of all those associated with the enterprise. In any event, the lion's share of the decision-making power and responsibility for decisions made have come to rest in the hands of the direktor. Exceptions do exist, but where they do, the economic performance of the enterprise is often so dismal that it is not possible to perceive those cases as being a challenge to the norm. One very illustrative example of nonproductive management friction is the steel industry in Skopje where production is incredibly low (in spite of a new foreign built and equipped plant) and where workers' groups have relentlessly asserted their management function. Production remains disastrously low which in turn invites political interference.

Yugoslav scholars—philosophers, industrial sociologists, and economists among them—have focused their attention on the management dilemma of direktors. An economist instructed me, "That the workers' council or the workers can make policy is naive and fundamentally wrong." He went on to say that although they cannot make or create policy they can choose between alternatives. He reiterated, "experience proves that the system does not work and cannot work as per the design." Because the workers' council has the power to establish the division of authority, there is a legal rationalization for their transferring or ceding power, or at least substantial latitude, to the direktor. Veljko Rus, Ljubljana philosopher, has done some impressive research into the organizational dimensions of the decentralized economy, and especially modern industrial organization. Basically, Rus' empirical work points to a correlation between optimal operation of the enterprises and the amount of power vested in the direktors. He posits that the "best" enterprises are those with the most managerial power. Rus' investigations are devoted mainly to the implications of the conflict between two thrusts of the reforms, the trend toward integration (rationalizing production through enterprises, that is, inter-firm consolidation) and the increase in participation.[14] Sociologist Rudi Supek is another scholar who has researched the enterprises from an organizational and functional perspective revealing the critical nature of the reforms to the systemic development of Yugoslavia.[15] In the past two years analytic and reflective articles have repeatedly appeared in Praxis, Politika, Ekonomska-

26

Politika, and Direktor. Their tone is often different, but the core of their message is consistent with the position stated above. The editor of another national publication suggested that, "the mythos of the workers' council being made up of the 'common' worker is completely false." It is composed of engineers, middle management, and informed workers who can cope with the difficult questions that come before them.

The direktors' own perceptions of their newly defined positions are illuminating. Three questions elicited the following selected responses—each from a different industry and section of the country. A precis of response follows. The words and phrases are verbatim but some editing of comments has been done without altering the nature of the respondent's meaning.

Question A: What is the functional relationship between the workers' council and the direktor ?

> Small groups direct the firm and supply spectacular ideas. These may be the management board, "syndicates," or the workers' council. The worker "pays" for all new ideas. The workers can and do buy special knowledge. The direktor must lead the company but must also prove success. Ideas come from educated people; the direktor uses these ideas and the workers' council accepts or approves them. In this way the workers have a check on progress, decisions, and business in general.
> Direktor of an Enterprise for Technological Consultation

> A good direktor has no trouble with the workers' council. If the direktor is weak he will occasionally be challenged by the Chairman of the workers' council. He prepares reports on important decisions. The reports must be clear. The sharpest challenge to the direktor's power comes not from the workers but from the middle range of petty technicians and foremen. Politics in its crudest form gets in this middle range. It is the old adage: a little bit of education is a dangerous thing—especially when coupled with great aspirations.
> Direktor of a Steel Enterprise

> The workers' council elects experts because they realize that this must be a "professional" group. Committees often have a greater role than the workers' council. They can make some decisions apart from the council. The unskilled worker occasionally present problems for

worker self-management. The function of workers' self-management is to make clear to the worker that the results depend on his work. Another way to put it, his income is dependent upon his efforts. Decisions must be presented to the workers' council in a professional way and the council can demand that a particular argument or position be prepared by the management. However, the council can and does so authorize officials of the enterprise to independently make some decisions thereby delegating or transferring its power. How much and how the direktor has power is a matter of the person of the manager—his approach and his success can substantially enhance his power. The direktor is, of course, elected by the workers' council but politics rarely plays a part. Economic or enterprise success is the measure.

Direktor of a Banking Enterprise

The workers' council must have the power. The direktor is the <u>executive</u>. On major issues (plans, major allocations) the direktor must have workers' council approval. There is a Yugoslav statute stating that the direktor must keep the law and is responsible for enterprise performance. In fact, in some contracts only the direktor is responsible. Direktors can make many many decisions. Their power is very very large. The councils <u>approve</u>, not make, policy but in this way do participate in the making.

Direktor of a Manufacturing Enterprise

The direktor governs technology and solves everyday problems. In our enterprise the direktor serves with three management boards (economic, general, technical) whose purpose it is to procure and present data to the workers. The direktor has the power to run the enterprise. It is easier to explain matters relating to the workers' economic relationship to the enterprise than it is to explain technological data, decisions, or programs. Worker participation has a definite and important function in terms of the individual's political and social involvement. Success in the firm makes harmony, harmony increases productivity, producitvity makes the direktor more secure in his position. The workers' council looks to the short-range; only the direktor sees the long-range.

Chairman of the Workers' Council of a Transport Enterprise

The people on the council are above the workers in capability and expertise. The entire enterprise must accept this expertise. All workers at all levels are interested in a better life and they understand that effective and innovative decisions must be made to accomplish the growth of the enterprise. Workers' council meetings are held about fifteen times a year, the direktor and a small group set the agenda and agree on materials to be distributed. When the enterprise runs badly the direktor is put out, when it runs well the direktor has a limited mandate.

Direktor of an Agricultural Enterprise

Presenting the data in this raw form may be less conducive to analytic conclusions but it does illustrate the thrust of more than one hundred conversations and interviews. In each there is a sense, at least to this analyst, of pragmatism accommodating principle. Real participation exists but the workers do not make policy. For perspective, few political scientists or other analysts would claim that the people in the United States actually make foreign or national policy.

Questions B and C: How is the management relationship (direktor-workers) affected by:

1. the advent and introduction of technology and technological decisions?
2. a commitment by the enterprise to joint investment involving foreign firms?

The responses to these questions were more consonant than those to the first. If the councils are to operate at all they must incorporate an ever-expanding body of technological awareness if not expertise. These necessary qualifications tend to solidify a management group in each enterprise whose propensity to communicate with and respond to the workers varies significantly. Some of the enterprises have a formula for the membership of their councils which includes non-expert categories, but it is impossible to conclude from such representation whether their role is a meaningful or merely symbolic one. In essence, the routines of the direktor and the council do not structurally change under the circumstances above, (1) and (2), yet functionally new demands create an acute need for increased authorization for the direktor to maintain his management efficacy. The advent of technology, at least in its initial stages, will create informational gaps between direktors and workers' councils and in turn between the councils and the workers. This phenomenon need not be permanent.

Nevertheless, it can be verified that it bears the potential for politically-directed conflict. One direktor concluded that, "the workers will become increasingly supportive [of the direktor] with the advent of complex technological developments and as long as the success of the enterprise is readily apparent to them." However, their loss of faith could spell trouble for "direktor and politicians alike." The same respondent posed the "summary problem" in these terms: "Expertise is prostitution when mixed with politics," illustrating his and most direktors' normative and professional apprehension about the role of politicians in the managerial development of the firm. Another suggested: "The real problem is the speed of development. In a management situation in which the workers are increasingly having choices and decisions put before them for which they have little background or understanding, the 'wish' of the system and the 'reality' of the system clash to produce conflict." In essence, gaps between theory and practice are generated by the inherent differences in education among managers and workers and by the pace of change and growth required for the enterprise to remain competitive in the modern world. These gaps generate conflict at the microlevel in the system.

An investment in technology is generally a long-range proposition. As noted earlier in the direktors' comments, with their perspective they are more likely to recognize the justification and credibility of such changes. The workers' council, however, has more difficulty with such a long-term perspective, especially given that short-term change affects them most severely. Unemployment, reeducation, relocation, and diminished wages (as a result of expanded investment) are all tangible short-term ramifications of much technological development in contemporary Yugoslavia. For these reasons managers and engineers can adjust more readily to innovation and are seldom as threatened by it as the workers may be. Nonetheless, nearly all Yugoslav enterprises have responded to challenges of the competitive market by looking toward technological advances. For most, this has involved the creation of and dependence on "expert management boards" whose function it is to apprise themselves of alternatives, produce plans for the enterprise, and guide complex issues of its policy.

"Joint investment" poses a second set of interrelationships which fundamentally modify the system. Seeking technology and capital, in that order, Yugoslav enterprises can now make contractual agreements with foreign firms which provide ownership and investment by the foreign enterprise. Under these arrangements of international and interenterprise management, the designed relationship between direktor and workers can become very strained. All interviewees agreed that the conditions of joint investment require the

deposition of greater power and latitude in the direktor's hands.
In fact, in some contracts he is singularly responsible in a legal
sense. Foreign investors generally seek two guarantees for their
participation: a measure of ownership and a significant role in management. The direktor's action can be restricted (1) by any explicit
workers' council restraints and (2) by the terms of the contract with
the foreign firm. Miodrag Sukijasovic, of the Institute of International
Economics and Politics, Belgrade, has undertaken an impressive
study of the new programs of foreign investment. His is a legal and
organizational (structural) examination which touches upon some of
the points under consideration here. For example, given that contractual commitments are often binding for some length of time,
issues which might have otherwise been fair game for the workers'
council at a future point in time do not find their way to a workers'
council agenda. Most joint investment arrangements provide for a
"joint operation board" (JOB) which generally works with few restrictions once the parties of the association initially constitute it and
grant it powers. As Sukijasovic explained it, the councils are further
restricted in their ability to distribute profits. "The workers' council
may dispose of the Yugoslav net profit," indicating, as this does,
that the operating expenses, foreign investor's percentage, federal
taxes less "incentive gradation," and automatic reinvestment percentage are first deducted from the gross receipts. In other words, the
domestic enterprise's share is "off the bottom" as opposed to "off
the top." The JOB is a curious mechanism designed to provide some
assurance to the foreign partner. The foreign firm has 50 per cent
representation on the board regardless of the percentage of investment. Patterns of decision-making are not yet well developed, but
a unanimity rule is common. Broached with the question of situations
in which a conflict arises and a decision must be made, indications
were, "It is a matter of mutual confidence but when an irresolvable
conflict develops, the decision is postponed, or more likely it is
referred to the two enterprise direktors for resolution." In response
to the question, "Do joint investment, advancing technology, and
modern management techniques limit, if not wholly restrict, workers'
council decision-making?" an academic acknowledged: "Such is a
technological and societal truth yet unproven specifically in foreign
business relations but certainly conceivable. The workers approve
more and more and the efficiency of the councils in an economic
sense is questionable." Ljubomir Veljkovic, editor-in-chief of Borba
and its weekly publication Ekonomska-Politika, pointed out that under
conditions of joint investment, "the workers are represented by their
direktor. It is a necessary functional arrangement." He also offered
the opinion, and a highly informed one at that, that joint investment

as a method of accumulating needed technology and capital would continue growing.

The essential point is that three distinct clusters of interests exist in the Yugoslav microeconomic relationship, each with its own economic and political priorities: the workers, the direktors, and the republic and national political leadership. Each has its own power base—the workers in the form of their labor and/or as potential political dissidents, the direktors as a store of badly needed expertise and a basic political support strata in the society, and the politicos as holders of policy-making authority and designers of the goals of systemic development. How the first two interact has been briefly discussed, after a concluding remark this examination turns to the linkages forged in the past few years between the last two.

All these features, many of them dynamic, of the Yugoslav enterprise system point increasingly to a changing role for the enterprise direktor. The change, while not sharp nor particularly consistent throughout the system, is nonetheless traceable and predictable. Generally, it seems that both the Socialist idealists and the practitioners are in agreement that ultimately something of the "classical" (non-Marxist) management relationship is needed to promote the growth and development of the economy. Essentially this transition is one from "bureaucratic" forms or systems of management toward "profit-motivated" or "growth-oriented" management. While it is a reform basically of the economic sector of the society, it may be the vanguard of changes cautiously contemplated (although less so every year) for the political system. And even if this is not the case, the success and momentum of the changes will be felt all the same in the political bureaucracies. It means that direktors as a group are a central force in the development of the socialist system of contemporary Yugoslavia, and it is to their linkage with the political system that we now turn.

NOTES

1. The main thrust of the American literature treats the Yugoslav system from the economist's perspective. A few citations are offered to illustrate the point:

E. Neuberger and E. James, "The Yugoslav Self-managed Enterprise," Stony Brook Working Paper #26, Economic Research Bureau, SUNY, January 1971.

Jan Vanek, The Behavior and Performance of Self-governing Enterprises under Worker's Management (2 volumes) unpublished manuscript.

Jaroslav Vanek, General Theory of Labor-Managed Marked Economics, Cornell University Press, New York, 1970.

Benjamin Ward, The Socialist Economy: A Study of Organizational Alternatives, Random House, New York, 1967.

2. N=98 direktors, smapled by this field research and data extracted from the full publishing run of Direktor, Privredni Pregled, Beograd, January 1969-January 1971, and from Ekonomska-Politika, Borba, Beograd, Najvecih, 1970, 1971, 1972, 1973.

3. Milovan Djilas as well as many other less prominent critics of fundamental organizational change in the Yugolsav system point to the "gray" area between initiative and autonomy in the name of socialist development, and capitalist entrepreneurship. Soviet official indictments are particularly harsh on this point. The current label for such trends is "anarcho-syndicalism."

4. A representative list of interviewees may be obtained on request from the author. The list includes government, academic, and enterprise officials. It should be added that the cooperation and patience with which this project was greeted were a tribute, in themselves, to the positive and sincere efforts toward development that are clear within Yugoslavia. It is in this same vein of critical self-evaluation that this writer represents some of those positions and attitudes of the contemporary economic elite. If at any time on the following pages a response (to one of the interview questions) seems simplistic or inappropriately terse it is likely a function of the translation or the fault of this writer. The single dominant impression that could be carried away from the numerous discussions with interviewees was that their responses were sophisticated and reflective.

5. "Political criteria" was interpreted by each interviewee. Little or no effort was made by this researcher to solidify or clarify the term. In all cases the respondent did differentiate between political and economic rationalizations for policy which was the essential distinction this aspect of the conversation was seeking to examine.

6. During the second six months of 1965 prices of manufactured goods rose by 143 percent resulting in a cost of living increase of 135 percent. Data and percentages from Yugoslav reports compiled in "Medjun-arodna politika," Beograd, Nemanjina 34, E/23, p. 2.

7. Themes are drawn from the Eighth Congress of the LCY and were echoed consistently by direktors and other officials in interview situations.

8. Official interpretations placed upon the controversial Amendment XV to the Federal Constitution.

9. Deborah D. Milenkovitch, Plan and Market in Yugoslav Economic Thought, Yale University Press, New Haven, 1971, p. 111.

10. Ibid.

11. Anthony Sylvester, "Management by Workers," Financial Times, April 26, 1971, p. 13.

12. Milenkovitch, op. cit., p. 115.

13. Numerous open and running battles between journalists and political figures highlighted the last half of 1969 and the first few months of 1970. Borba, Politika, and Ekonomska-Politika all were involved in and carried accounts of the rift. These were indicative of such exchanges to be found in the majority of republic capitals.

14. Veljko Rus, "Samoupravni egalitarizam i drustvena diferencijacija," Praxis, Hrvatsko Filosofsko Drustvo, Zagreb, September-December 1969, Year IV, No. 5/6, pp. 811-27. (Other research by Rus is synthesized in this article.)

15. A representative article by Supek may be found in M. J. Broekmeyer (ed.), Yugoslav Workers' Self-Management, D. Reidel Publishing Co., Dordrecht, Holland, 1970, entitled, "Problems and Perspectives of Workers' Self-Management in Yugoslavia," pp. 216-42.

3

INTERESTS OF THE
ECONOMIC SECTOR AND
POLICY-MAKERS

One of the most easily crystallized of the relationships between the economy and the polity is the linkage for interest articulation by the economic elite to the policy-making elite via the network of representative chambers. The <u>Savezne Privredni Komore</u> (SPK; translated as either Federal Chamber of Commerce or Federal Chamber of Economy) is the central representative organization of the economic sector of the state at the national level. Its place and role in the whole system is very fluid. That it has a real role, however, and the potential for an even greater one, is unmistakable. Yet lack of stability and the widely disparate opinions of the place and future of the chamber have protected it from an academic examination. Precisely these factors make the subject more interesting.

The delegation of <u>formal</u> powers to the SPK does not help much in describing either its actual function or that which its originators envisioned for it. Consequently, the entire network of chambers which model themselves on the SPK at the republic, district, and local levels is characterized by flexibility, uncertainty, and ambiguity. Many chambers so confronted have carved out their own shapes not always in line with and often critical of the SPK. For these reasons the data from the interview research may be used to examine some of the general functions of the SPK and the various republican economic chambers. Even more fluid and ill-defined is the relationship between the government and the SPK and its members. A diversity of opinions and a few brief but illustrative cases are presented on the following pages to illuminate both the process and difficulties of the relationship.

Above all, the SPK is a very loose organization which serves to channel some interests of various economic sectors (1) to the federal officials and (2) to the other economic sectors. The way and the enthusiasm with which the chamber approaches this function is a subject for examination. A bit more difficult and considerably more general is the problem of portraying the current "power" position of the SPK in the overall political-economic system of Yugoslavia. The field project began with the hypothesis taken from the literature that the SPK's functional role in the system was (1) to control the growth, direction, and development of the economic sector; (2) to initiate economic policy; (3) to monitor change and systemic problems; (4) to establish and issue plans and industry guidelines; and (5) to funnel interests, demands, and supports from the enterprises, industries, and republics to the political leadership. This interwoven set of objectives is consistent with the structural design of the government, but beyond that, given the flexibility to designate priorities among the above it appeared to be in line with the impetus and commitment of the political forces toward a more open and responsive system. Appropriately, the first of all the interviews was with a Secretary of the SPK in Belgrade. The first question put to him was: Which of the above is the primary purpose of the chamber? As it happened the whole of his response was a precis of both the opinions of over two dozen other chamber personnel and of the interviewees at large. His moderate assessment was put in this framework. "The chamber organizes and coordinates; it can initiate, it can funnel interests, but more than anything else it balances the centralized and decentralized elements in the system." In retrospect his response was a politic answer par excellence. He did not overstate the case. Rather he alluded to the fact that it does organize and coordinate some delegated responsibilities and, "more than anything else," is caught in between two very strong and juxtaposed strains in the political make-up of the contemporary state. That is all he really said and, from a purist's perspective, that is all there is to be said.

He did suggest that the chamber "represents the interests of the economy by coordinating economic and societal interests." When asked if the SPK could be called the "highest collective voice of the economy," he cautiously reformulated the question in his response by labelling it: "the supreme specifically economic organization." The distinction may be too subtle, but his emphasis is on the structure as opposed to the function of the body. His response left this investigator with the suspicion (later validated) that one would find many linkages of an informal nature.

When the enterprises represented in Belgrade find a consensus that a legal or political change is needed, what is the procedure? "The President of the SPK takes the proposal to the Federal Chamber." This and many other statements adequately indicated that the SPK is not commonly a policy-generating body. It is more accurately a "transmission belt" of political interests, demands, and supports of the economic sector. This should be qualified by the point that in the realm of economic policy of limited scale and of an essentially nonpolitical nature, the SPK has some policy-generating latitude.

At the nucleus of the chamber there are a series of councils whose composition is drawn along industrial lines. Not all Yugoslav enterprises are represented in the SPK. Criteria are applied to select those enterprises which will delegate a person to represent that enterprise in Belgrade. The councils are proportionately represented in the chamber's assembly and from this assembly the SPK President and the Management Board are elected (see Figure 1). Planning is done in practice by an "expert and experienced group." When queried on the source of the original impetus for the economic reforms, the Secretary replied, "not the SPK; experts were behind the changes"; a most interesting formulation for an officer of the Chamber. Thus the search for the effective channels of articulation began with skepticism about the mechanisms in the system for absorbing and accommodating such interests of the economic sector. Yet substantive policy appeared relatively consistent with these interests; sharp political conflict was lacking between political and economic elites and Yugoslav periodical sources often pointed to a prolific intercourse between the two groups. Subsequently, it was hypothesized that routine channels do exist and that these are a critical factor in charting the economic and political movements of the system. This segment of the research held the potential for spotlighting (1) the political priority held by the economic sector, (2) their political adroitness and "clout," (3) the nature and magnitude of the issues (interests) pressed by the managers, and (4) the general pattern for articulation, aggregation, and communication in the system. The economic chamber is the point of departure for this examination.

Direktor's and officials' assessments of the activities or nonactivities of the SPK turn out to have little meaning in terms of the overall liberal-conservative political postures of these key elites. No pattern or correlation seems to have developed, adding credence to a hypothesis tested at some length in the following section that no correlation exists between direktors' "business policy" and their "politics." This distinction, not always subtle, clearly makes them less effective as a solidified political force, but it also partially shelters or insulates them as a group from politically-directed attack or criticism.

The opinions which follow have been selected because they represent the range and distribution of the positions taken on the functions, power, position, and problems of the chamber at the Federal level. The source of most of these statements is an enterprise direktor of a major firm or chairman of a workers' council who was a member of the SPK's elite Management Board when the research

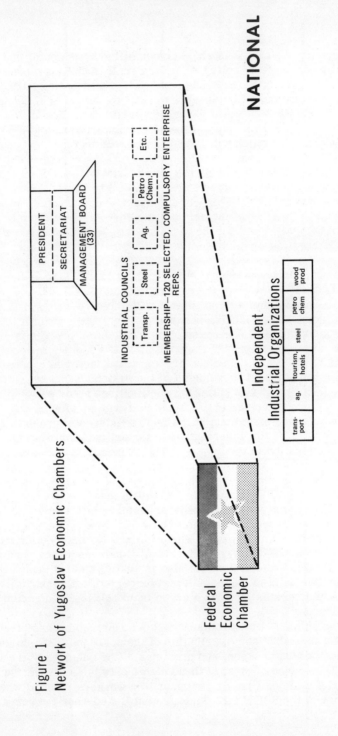

Figure 1
Network of Yugoslav Economic Chambers

PRESIDENT

SECRETARIAT

MANAGEMENT BOARD
(33)

INDUSTRIAL COUNCILS

Transp. | Steel | Ag. | Petro Chem. | Etc.

MEMBERSHIP—120 SELECTED, COMPULSORY ENTERPRISE REPS.

NATIONAL

Independent
Industrial Organizations

| trans-port | ag. | tourism, hotels | steel | petro chem | wood prod |

Federal
Economic
Chamber

38

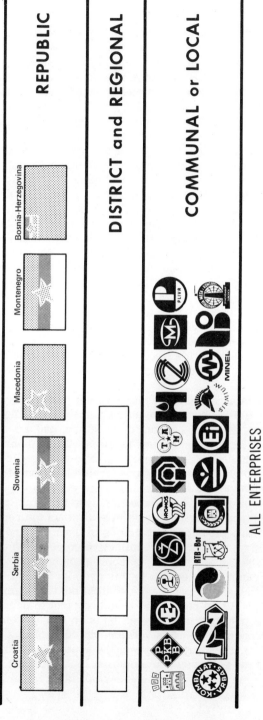

REPUBLIC

DISTRICT and REGIONAL

COMMUNAL or LOCAL

Croatia Serbia Slovenia Macedonia Montenegro Bosnia-Herzegovina

ALL ENTERPRISES

Library of Davidson College

was conducted.[1] Beginning at the positive end of the continuum, interviewees made very strong assertions of the SPK's position. For example, pursuant to a statement of the chamber's great influence, "the government must listen to the SPK in some cases because of the potential political repercussions of its unresponsiveness." A more specific statement was forthcoming from another direktor: "The SPK has a broad range of functions depending on the time, issue, and political sensitivity. The councils handle much of the intra-industry policy while the expertise of the chamber is increasingly called upon to advise the government." Contradictions sharpen as cases become more specific. For example, one direktor indicated that the government is not fundamentally an economic policy maker. Such policy, he explained, is made by the industrial councils and the SPK. However, when pressed on the single most vital interest of the transport enterprise, he pointed to the federally-established rates whose level is established by a unit outside the chamber (Federal Institute of Prices, discussed further on). The same is true for many of the more strictly and centrally controlled industries—iron and steel, agriculture, petrochemicals, and transportation. The precipitant opinion of many direktors was that the SPK was listened to on economic matters, yet their explanations cast doubt or, at the very least, called for qualification on this very proposition. Some mentioned the Federal Secretariat for Economic Affairs, a government bureaucracy, as a store of expert opinion on the economy which rivals the SPK.

A round table discussion with four very impressive members of the Bosnia-Herzegovina Economic Chamber, including the President, Secretary, Foreign Economic Secretary, and a prominent direktor, produced yet another slant on the question. Their emphasis was on the embryonic nature of the chambers. The end product of the slow metamorphosis which they envisioned would be a set of fully independent chambers empowered to decide all economic questions. However, in the realm of the contemporary system, the SPK's power is restricted to those situations (rare indeed) when the representatives in the Federal Chamber are unanimous in their demands for change. Under these circumstances, the collective voice of the economy has much power and the SPK can make some economic policy. A few tangible programs lend support to this premise. The interviewees were adamant about the propensity of the Federal Chamber to propose "real" change. "Up to now the SPK had no right to demand or make change but the power of independent decision and agreement is theirs."

The "economic power in agreement" concept is a vulnerable one. It appears true that, in spite of the nonbinding nature of SPK decisions and the voluntary participation in SPK programs, its leadership in innovation and development is real, if irregular. The network of functioning economic chambers must be examined since the reforms seem to have effectively insulated its debates and decisions from direct Party control at all levels. From the empirical data, the pecking order for economic policy matters at the national level seems to take on the patterns of Figure 2. The SPK's greatest influence and power are concentrated over (in ascending order) (1) planning, (2) policy and guidelines for particular industries, and (3) introduction of innovative technological and management programs. More profound and encompassing policy is yet beyond its given functional authority.

The SPK is not without its detractors, some outspoken. Theirs is a persuasive case with the weight of much empirical evidence and numerous case studies. The issue of basic steel prices is an example. In 1969 the issue was a pressing one and the SPK took up discussion of it. As one engineer put it, "the 'agreement principle' made the SPK ineffective.[2] Disagreement is expected and natural between steel producers and steel buyers—the vast majority of the enterprises represented." For the chamber the problem was irresolvable and this indecisiveness resulted in the abdication of power and influence to government agencies. Nevertheless, this same engineer commented that the "politicians" look at the SPK very skeptically and cautiously because it bears "so much power." By this he indicated he meant potential political power by virtue of its broad, representative, and essential base of support for the system. In the decentralized system these are the men with the "grass-roots" ties.

Anchoring the negative end of the scale was a comment by a long time Party leader, government official, and academic. His opinion painted a dim picture. "The political powers are not responsive to the SPK. Chamber meetings can impose sanctions within the economic community but the government can exercise free play on the basis [rationale] of the need to protect the public interest from the economic interest." This is a very illuminating formulation, especially since it is consistent with the political apprehensions vis-à-vis the economic elite found in the politics of many Communist systems.

The predominant factors in the system now are those which detract from the political power of the SPK. A brief review of these factors follows. First is the condition of compulsory membership which, while forcing all eligible enterprises into one body, works counter to the principle of "agreement" in the chamber, often rendering it ineffective. The Economic Chamber in Slovenia has eliminated the compulsory membership provision with some success. Rudi Kolak, SPK President from 1970 to 1972 was known to be considering such changes. There was widespread speculation throughout the economic community about changes (some with political overtones) which were actively discussed under the leadership of Kolak. Most

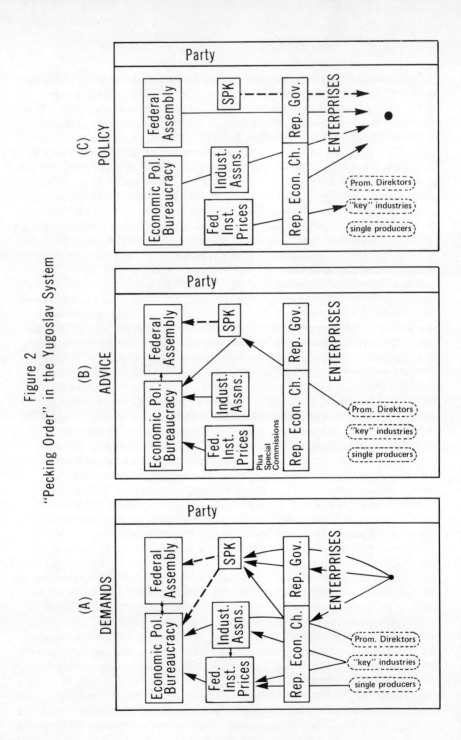

Figure 2
"Pecking Order" in the Yugoslav System

42

enterprise direktors characterized him as an "innovator." Yugoslav analysts speculated about a "new look" including smaller "action" groups to counter some of the heterogeneity and weak administration. Second are the divisions of interest which are evident (a) among re-publics, (b) between essentially service and transport sectors and the production sectors, and (c) between producers and consumers of basic commodities. This constitutes a very real difficulty, one which often polarizes and thereby freezes SPK action on an issue. Third, the existence of numerous separately organized and directed industrial associations (interest groups) has detracted substantially from the influence and power of the SPK by serving as the alternate and effective vehicle for pressing demands, making requests, and confronting the government with arguments. These groups exist in nearly every significant industry or service sector. Among the most effective are the Iron and Steel Federation, the National Bankers' Association, the Community of Railways, the Council for Flat Development and Engineering, and a number of groups representing agricultural inter-ests.

Finally, the Economic Chamber's expertise is duplicated and challenged by a network of special "institutes" and "commissions," some formally government affiliated, whose function is to generate policy recommendations and assessments independent of the SPK. As a result of these and other factors, the SPK is often not the initiator of reforms or changes. This record of inertia and lack of leadership has created an image of the organization which detracts in very real ways from its potential political power and societal role.

This potential, the alternative directions and functions for the future, is a primary subject of controversy within the system. The range of opinions and ideas held by central figures in Yugoslavia itself is nearly overwhelming. Some analysts (all participants in the system) picture the SPK of the near future as a buffer between the economy and the government, serving to keep politics out of the economic realm. Others see it as an increasingly rationalized, effec-tive, and congealed voice of the decentralized economy bringing reform and pluralism upon the political elite. Still others predict the complete demise of the organization—destined to wallow in the mediocrity and pettiness of perspectiveless conflicts. It is clearly an area worthy of closer investigation and which might bear a clue to the destiny of the entire system. In a policy sense, then, the economic chamber as an institution is only an occasional vehicle for interest articulation and aggregation or for rule application and political communication. The political leadership responsible for economic policy, to be found largely in the Federal Executive Committee, has more direct channels for the dissemination and administration of policy decisions than through the SPK. Among these are the Federal Assembly, the special

TABLE 2

Elite Opinion of the Federal Chamber of Economy (SPK)

Question: Generally, in view of the strengths and weaknesses of the SPK we have discussed, how would you characterize (that is, assess) the immediate future of the SPK?	Direktors	SPK Representatives	Economic Chamber Personnel— Republic Level	Other Government Officials	Chairmen, Workers' Councils and Others	Total
I: Ineffective, strife torn	12	0	2	0	2	16
II: Highly limited, minor issues	39	7	4	3	6	59
III: Buffer between economy and government	6	2	0	1	0	9
IV: Improved and effective voice of decentralized economy	9	3	0	2	3	17
V: Very strong policy organ	0	0	0	0	0	0
No response	13	0	1	0	1	15
Total	79	12	7	6	12	116

Source: Compiled by the author.

44

commissions, including the Federal Institute of Prices, and less commonly, the Party. These linkages illustrated in Figure 2 have become significantly less critical with the growth of the powers and responsibilities of the economic chambers and executive committees on the republic level. If communication and interpersonal linkages are adequate indicators, the increase in the policy-making scope of the subnational units has not been accompanied by a significant increase in the relationship or coordination between the Federal and republic levels. In other words, it does not appear that the decentralization of economically relevant policy-making is a facade. The republics' chambers and governments are not a new detour through which Federal policy is channeled. Because of these changes and the breadth of microresponsibility in the economic sector, a devolution has taken place in the frequency of contact between the prominent political elite circles and the collective enterprise leadership. This direction of change in the system requires a rethinking of the assumption implied earlier that it is a pressing objective of the economic sector to establish effective access to the national political leadership. At the very least, given this reversal in the propensity of the ranking national elite to routinely make pervasive economic policy, the effort to solidify these linkages has subsided in large measure.

The mechanisms for submitting advice to the upper echelons of the system or for pressing demands and needs is hardly a passé subject. In one sense, the task of establishing the enterprise's (or industry's) political position has become more consuming by virtue of the fact that there are now two clearly delineated policy-formulating institutions, one at the republic level, the other at the national level. The direktors must concern themselves with their "influence" at both points (levels) in the matrix of government.

Patterns of political influence can be clearly differentiated if "advice" and "demands" are dealt with separately. The sources from which the policy elites elicit advice and consultation are quite restricted. At the republic level one will often find a club-like approach to evaluating policy and its ramifications. Put in yet a different way, a select group of prominent direktors seems to emerge; a tight circle of experienced men to whom pending problems and decisions will be circulated in advance of the taking of final measures. Though in differing proportions in the six republics, this pattern does not seem to vary in any predictable fashion. For example, it is not clear that the circle is tighter or better defined in the "underdeveloped" republics than it is in the more economically "advanced" republics or vice versa. At the Federal level in Yugoslavia the policy generating bureaucracy and its leadership gather opinions and suggestions from a slightly wider cross-section. A formalized network of commissions exists at the highest level of Federal government to serve the immediate informational needs of the decision-makers. Their functions and areas of responsibility are ill-defined, but in each of the economically relevant commissions there is a parameter of substantive concern. The most prominent of these is the Federal Institute of Prices, the name of which implies its focus of responsibility. Institutes and commissions are usually semiofficial in nature and are composed of a mixture of academics, direktors, officials, and other analysts whose expertise is credible. With few exceptions all are politically conservative in terms of commitment to Party and noninclination toward rapid change of the entire social system. But in terms of the policy areas on which they are called upon to render advice, they defy classification except to suggest that collectively their commitment to "development" exceeds their inclination toward the inflexible maintenance of the political pattern or complexion of the state. This was revealed consistently in interview situations. While a matter of constant legitimate concern, system maintenance could be subordinated to innovative long-term programs if the potential yield of those programs seemed credible enough.

Other sources of advice are (1) the industrial associations of firms sharing a single productive or service function, and whose organization and longevity are quite impressive in some cases, and (2) highly visible or outstanding direktors. These channels for the most part are not regularized. Intermittent at best, they are extremely difficult to examine in any kind of rigorous manner.

Demands in a system so fundamentally changing are injected from nearly every quarter, as one might expect. The "testing" of channels by principals (direktors and other relatively local elites) is quite clearly in evidence. Nonetheless, patterns or sequences have emerged which make charting possible but not definitive. In general, enterprises funnel "demands"—politically relevant preferences and desires—through either the political and economic chambers at the republic level or through the SPK. Marked exceptions (noted on Figure 3.2) can be recognized in the path used by "special groups" in the economic sector. For example, some prominently established, well-connected, or accomplished direktors have linkages directly with the Federal bureaucracy. Industries formerly identified as "key" industries typically have more firmly institutionalized industrial associations and in some cases a clear rapport with central organizations of authority like the Federal Institute of Prices. Finally, there is another group, "single producer" enterprises, which may be labelled monopoly producers. Because of their extraordinary nature and position in the economy, these have very well-oiled linkages with critical federal policy-generating institutes and commissions. The SPK is relatively ineffective in the face of such direct "influence" linkages. It is slower, more cumbersome, and less

46

emphatic by virtue of the compromise intrinsic to "agreement," assuming it can act to press demands at all. It should be duly noted, however, that its impotence is largely a function of its structural design as an organization. Organizational rules and procedural changes could alleviate many such barriers to effective articulation of interests. If only in terms of their broad delivery of support and their potentially disruptive capability, the raw power of the direktors acting in concert is impressive. This political muscle appears to be flexed with significant success on the republic and local levels.

Consonant with the entire picture portrayed by Figure 3.2, the SPK has maneuvered ever so cautiously in defining its role in the overall system. Time will judge the wisdom of such a reserved development and assertion of political power. Some judgments, if qualified adequately, are possible. The hesitation of the SPK to become aggressive in a policy-making or policy-influencing sense has disillusioned and frustrated some of the most dynamic men in the economic system. The lack of confidence expressed in the interview statements of the members of the Management Board is adequate evidence of an erroding faith in the organization. Interestingly, the pragmatism which looms as a progressive guide to enterprise leadership on virtually all other levels of economic activity in Yugoslavia seems to be absent in the conduct and deliberation of the Chamber. The SPK has few routinized channels of access to seats of decisional responsibility in the system. It continues to dwell in the areas of ceded authority, which suggests that it is not a challenge to the political elite and has little inclination to become one. This is most vividly clear if one is considering fundamental policy changes. The councils, the Chamber, and the Management Board are more vocal and more active on relatively limited policy issues.

In the face of all these limitations and negative dimensions of SPK behavior, the economic sector remains the most critical mass in an at best uncertain, at worst explosive political situation in the 1970s. As most contemporary analysts of Yugoslav politics have emphasized, the system is laboring, with mixed success, to weld the heterogeneous segments of the society together. However, the magnitude and implication of these basic schisms among the national, ethnic, and religious groups have been challenged most prominently in the work of M. George Zaninovich and Gary K. Bertsch.[3] Their empirical evidence is reasonably convincing and is in line with both the interview data accumulated by this project and with more subjective impressions gathered throughout Yugoslavia. Its basic premise is that, considering the range of variables which are relevant in terms of political behavior, Yugoslavs are not as heterogeneous as their superficial identifications might indicate. This established, one contrasting variable is stressed. The level of economic development—investment, production, standard of living, average annual income, natural and human resources—remains a most visible, sore, and politically volatile reality. It is essential that the political system recruit and retain the commitment of the micro and macroeconomic leadership in the amelioration of tensions. The Chambers in the republic capitals have thrown their support behind this effort on the rationale that whatever develops the Yugoslav domestic market is, in the long run, beneficial to the producers. The SPK has likewise extended its support. The essential point is that the momentum of the Chambers' commitment has been enough to mollify thrusts against the financial and technological support of the underdeveloped regions emanating from the more aggressive and economically sound firms throughout the system. In this respect the support of the network of economic chambers had been invaluable to the political leadership. The same is true of the industrial associations, but their support is considerably more restrained.

SUMMARY

The political potential of the economic chambers as a policy relevant institution is great. With the decentralization of policy authority, the shift to more "responsive" as opposed to "control" social mechanisms, and the theoretical acceptance of market forces in the economy, a pattern of theoretically consistent and single direction reforms has been introduced whose logical corollary vis-à-vis the representative chambers is to endow them with a more active and central role in the system. The restraints on this development have been presented in this chapter. By way of review, they are:

1. compulsory membership of enterprises
2. the "agreement principle" with its organizational and decision-making problems, wherein there is no method of resolving the inherent conflicts of a body which represents the full crosssection of economic functions in the system
3. conservative political apprehension about the conflict defined in Marxian terms between the "public interests" and the "economic interests"
4. the duplication of functional channels for both upward and downward communication from the economic elite to the political elite
5. the caution of the chamber leadership born of bureaucratic experience and political memories which produces an acquiesced subservience to the Federal Chamber—the political chamber

48

The friction between the development and the devolution of the SPK and its counterparts at the republic and local levels would indeed appear to be one of the less apparent but acute indicators of the course of systemic change in socialist Yugoslavia. It is an ever heightening rift because no decisive moves have been taken. The "wait and see" syndrome typical of bureaucratic inertia and governmental lethargy is prevalent in and around the SPK. Yet the demands and needs of the economic system become more pressing with the advent of inflation, a balance of payments problem (in spite of dramatic gains through increased Yugoslav exports), and the ever growing need for broad entrepreneurial latitude coupled, somewhat paradoxically, with government policy financially and organizationally supporting such efforts through accommodative policy. Conclusions beyond those presented at this point in time would be speculative. However, venturing into that realm, the pressures to fill the informational, communicative, and policy-generating needs of the economic sector appear more enduring, more commensurate with the political and social direction of the system than do those restraints which detract from the capability of the Chamber.

The predominant factor which challenges all propositions about the nature of the system in Yugoslavia is its dynamic quality. As an experiment with distinct implications for both the structure and behavior of the system, the organizational, personnel, ideological, and collective dimensions of developments in Yugoslavia must come under some scrutiny before we can afford the luxury of any degree of confidence with regard to this charting of Yugoslav affairs. With these concerns foremost, one is invited to examine a wide variety of variables to be found in Chapter 4—National Economic Programs and Political Capability.

NOTES

1. The Management Board has a membership of between 30 and 35 members appointed by the Chamber assembly and charged with limited decisional authority and responsibility for policy execution. The Board is directed by the President of the Chamber. Generally, this is a prestigious and capable group of prominent direktors and officials of organized institutes and economic organizations. The Management Board is assisted by "expert committees and commissions."

2. This is the principle which is an operational and formal rule in the SPK. It requires unanimity for a major decision to be taken.

3. G. Bertsch and M. G. Zaninovich, "Centralization vs. Decentralization in Yugoslav Society," Panel paper presented to the APSA, Chicago 1971.

4

NATIONAL ECONOMIC PROGRAMS AND POLITICAL CAPABILITY: PROGRAMS AND DIRECTIONS OF DEVELOPMENT

As used in this study the term "national economic programs" is not restricted to governmental economic policy. Rather the more typical genre of program is extra-governmental (although sanctioned), and while "national" in scope, affects only selected sectors of the economy. This examination is restricted to the identification of trends and directions of change. Such a limitation is a function of the fluid nature of the systemic relations under scrutiny. A second word of explanation is essential. "Political capability" here is interpreted most broadly in order to facilitate the selection of those variables which this project has identified as central from all of those which affect or restrict the system's potential or active policy-generating function.

This chapter is an effort to draw together five distinct dimensions of the economy which in the total design of this study will contribute to the analysis of the policies of economic decision-making at the national (all Yugoslav) level. It provides a base for the discussion in Chapter 5 of foreign economic policy, especially that which is explicitly enterprise and republic initiated but which also implicitly points to federal government policy.

The importance of the political developments which revolve around economic policy, growth, and change create a need to focus on selected dimensions in which we have a particular interest and then to find indicators of both the direction and magnitude of change. These two tasks are highly interrelated and reflect in measure the kinds of data available as much as a calculated methodological design. Five dimensions will be examined: (1) organizational development; (2) personnel changes; (3) ideological transformations; (4) a residual category of indicators; and (5) shifts in publishing and research. As conceptualized each is a hybrid, and an effort will be made to describe new systemic features and thereby to prescribe the general direction of the system's development.

51

ORGANIZATIONAL DEVELOPMENTS

In this section new organizational entities, both government and privately initiated, are briefly examined. This is done on the assumption that such newly created associations reflect the needs and/or objectives of the economic sector. It may further be asserted that in some of the instances discussed, at the very least, passive acceptance by the political establishment has been crucial to their embryonic growth. Examples will help support the previous two propositions. The five specific cases below represent different levels of effort at organizational remodeling within the system—local, regional, national, and international—as well as varying structural approaches. Yet the overriding objective is the same for all: to rationalize (in a business sense) and sophisticate the particular target unit to nurture greater productivity, and to enhance its ability to compete in the present and future environments.

At the international level a number of organizational entities have been established, most of which are on the pattern of the International Investment Corporation for Yugoslavia (IICY). The IICY is a London based operation which has as its purpose the dissemination throughout Western Europe of specific information about Yugoslav investment potential and trade sources. It also directs inquiries relating to markets, financing, negotiations, and disputes to appropriate channels. The IICY was organized in early 1970 to promote joint business ventures and cooperation between "autonomous Yugoslav enterprises in industry, mining, tourism, and agriculture" and foreign firms. It is a nongovernmental operation with charter "shareholders" that include fifteen leading Yugoslav banks, the International Finance Corporation of the World Bank, and forty banks from Western Europe, Japan, and the United States.[1] With this backing it has become, in its short life, an aggressive yet sound foundation for the expansion of economic relations and the absorption of capital, technology, and management skills.

The IICY works on a project by project basis. Its accomplishments are impressive. It has completed or initiated joint ventures in the automobile, nonferrous metals, pulp and paper, chemical and petro-chemical industries. None of the projects have proven financially unsound. The capital costs of ongoing projects range from just below $5 million to over $100 million.

One project, and in some ways the most impressive undertaking, is the Dunlop (U.K.)-Fadip agreement. Dunlop's fixed investment amounts to £250,000 or $620,000. It is the first direct investment by a British firm in Yugoslavia since the Second World War and illustrates the fact that Yugoslavia offers attractive business investments for highly developed Western firms. The arrangement is one of give-and-take with specific and complementary advantages for both firms. Dunlop will participate in the formation of an enterprise for the production of wire braided hose to establish a position in the expanding Yugoslav market. It also can use its presence in Yugoslavia as a base from which to export to other less accessible Eastern European markets and to some developing countries for example, India, Chile, Kenya, Lebanon, Libya, Tunisia, and Pakistan, with which Yugoslavia has exceptional relations—a function of her positive political, as well as trade, relations. The parent company, Fadip of Becej, Yugoslavia, acquires Dunlop's technological expertise as well as its management capabilities through the latter's active participation in the new Yugoslav enterprise. Furthermore, Fadip can anticipate marketing assistance from Dunlop throughout the world. In this particular case the IICY took an active role in the negotiations between Fadip and Dunlop and contributed 19.3 percent of the fixed investment.[2]

Such deals are significant and are dealt with more fully in Chapter 5. However, the organization itself is a real departure from the traditional (1945-65) mode of economic intercourse with the West. The confidence and stability which have resulted from such international, nongovernmental financing are credible signs of economic growth and development. The nature of the shareholding arrangement and the partners of the organization mark the relative permanence of the IICY's contribution.

These same factors also indicate the development of patterns which are politically significant. The domestic economic growth of the Yugoslav system is linked to the financial backing of economic establishments from non-Communist states. While it is true that this portion is indeed very small (a mere 29 joint ventures as of April 1971), the commitment to and need for such assistance is important. A more subtle but no less real influence is the nurturing of a generally "profit-motivated" economic system. It is no longer taboo (politically or economically) to formulate a policy in these terms. The emphasis has been on the "hard" business wisdom of investment in Yugoslavia. Other political implications will be discussed in a review at the end of this section.

The organizational counterpart to the IICY in the United States is the Yugoslav American Corporation. It has its offices in New York and places an emphasis on joint agricultural and semiindustrial ventures.

Another organization new to the Yugoslav scene, yet quite impressive in its international credentials, is the Center for Industrial Organization and Development. Slobodan Ristic assumed leadership of this Belgrade association in the late 1960s. Its creation was a product of recommendations made by the Institute for Economic Research, a prestigious Yugoslav economic "brain trust" directed by the prominent scholar, Branko Horvath. As with the IICY, no government action or legal provisions were involved in the establishment of the organization. It came into being when a number of voluntary "founders" made the decision to associate loosely for the purpose of collectively accumulating and disseminating management expertise. The original group included the SPK, a small number of large and medium size Yugoslav enterprises (all industrial), and a select group of consultant/experts. The first two groups were conceived as the "recipients" or consumers of the suggestions of the experts. In the event that outside funding was lacking they, the enterprises, would also absorb the costs of the services. The consultant/experts were organized into a Board of Directors which also included representatives from the principal enterprises. A United Nations Project Manager serves as a nonvoting member of this board. The distinct objective of the group is to provide a consulting service which can deal with the problem of improving management techniques through more effective industrial organization and the realistic establishment of objectives on an enterprise scale. The decentralization reforms make this consultation critical. The United Nations committed itself (via UNESCO) to providing "intellectual" support for the project, which in practice will mean that American consultants will be sent to participate in the project under UN auspices. A modest UN grant was secured to "seed" the project.

In an interview with Ristic, formerly a Secretary with the Economic Chamber, he made the point that, while the organization was in its infancy, the development of this type of facility was indeed a departure from the system's previous approach to management and sources of management expertise. He explained that the Center had no political purpose and was entirely outside the governmental structure. This, in itself, is a point of contrast with what has become the "classical" Communist pattern of political and economic linkages. This organization is one clearly built upon the enterprise autonomy established by the Reforms. Specifically, the new endowment of authority made possible decisions that a common need existed, and that such a tactical organization was the optimal method for securing the desired expertise. That such consultation comes essentially from the West, and in particular from the United States, is unimportant to those involved in this efficiency-motivated quest. Its key political meaning is that such an "opening" is not perceived by the political establishment as either threatening or inconsistent with political policy or doctrine.

The Center should be viewed as an effort at the national level to improve specific aspects of industrial development by drawing on the Western experience in organization and management. Its potential as a "clearing house" of management consultation and organizer of seminars and management education is well established. Beyond this it is a proof of the flexibility given to the economic sectors by the ruling elite, and its bears potential as yet another device for the economic interests to insulate themselves and their immediate needs from politics.

The propositions made above are reinforced by the numerous programs and cooperative efforts which Yugoslavia has undertaken on the official level, including qualified participation in OECD and the EEC. These subjects are also developed more thoroughly in Chapter 5.

Sub-national efforts in the direction of fundamental reorganization schemes have also had visible effect on the economic sector and the system as a whole. From the field survey, it may be concluded that the wide variety of experiments with supra-enterprise economic organization were stimulated solely by the principals in those respective organizations. The impetus was theirs, and the latitude was theirs through a conscious and expeditious set of decisions by the political powers not to challenge or in any significant way impinge on the independent course of the enterprises and on their newly emerging entrepreneurial leadership.

The generic title for the product of most such reorganizational efforts is "community of interests." The precise number of these associations is difficult to establish because of the varying degree of formal organization among them. Suffice it to say, they are increasingly prevalent in the bulk of inter-enterprise relations in the more "developed" republics of Yugoslavia. Some are organized exclusively for economic advantages in the market; others with the additional design of more effective articulation of politically targeted (policy-targeted) needs and interests. Examples of the latter type are especially interesting. There is a tendency for this dual purpose type organization to develop in those economic sectors which are at either end of the liberal-conservative spectrum—the least and most "supervised" by the central authorities. Conservative industries are economic "backbone" areas such as agriculture, iron and steel, and transport while liberal industries tend to be less essential and technology-intensive.

Interviews were conducted with the leadership of each of these kinds of "communities." As the "Community of Railways" was discussed with key figures in that organization it was abundantly clear that the organization, whose membership is ostensibly voluntary but functionally mandatory of all rail enterprises run on the republic level, was constructed for three purposes—economic, semipolitical, and purely political. First, as an economic organization it was and is to communicate and coordinate (negotiate if necessary) the various rail enterprises to insure that the system runs effectively. Mundane

TABLE 3

Interest and Commitment to Supra-Enterprise and Inter-Enterprise Economic Organization

Question:* Does your enterprise have an interest in or involvement with any of these forms of inter-enterprise or supra-enterprise organization?	Positive Responses by Type of Organizational Interest					
	I Mergers (Organization integration)	II Community of Interests	III Industrial Associations	IV Joint Ventures	V No Interest	Total
Direktors						
Agricultural and Light Industry	7	12	9	4	3	35
Heavy Industry	6	13	17	10	4	50
Services	2	9	5	5	0	21
Others	0	3	1	3	0	7
Total	15	37	32	22	7	113

*Multiple responses possible.

Source: Compiled by the author.

56

considerations fall within this category, including scheduling and standardization of procedures. However, the railroads have increasingly used the organization as a forum to introduce technological change and industrial development. The introduction of piggyback service, "commercialization" of the system (improving public relations and advertising), and speculation about new rail lines to developing ports and industrial centers are examples. Second, as a semipolitical Community it is used as the central railway authority which negotiates and makes contracts with foreign rail companies. This is represented as a "semipolitical" purpose because traditionally (in both Communist and major Western European states) such a purpose is a guarded responsibility of the government. This responsibility of the Community of Railways has many political implications not the least of which is that those who control the Community can give preferential emphasis to international rail linkages for their own relatively developed areas. This could have the effect of increasing the gap between the republics. In practice, however, while a problem does exist on this score and rail service to many regions is unimpressive and growth-inhibiting, the Community leadership is committed to the "opening" of many of Yugoslavia's yet remote areas. It is of interest that this appears to be predicated on an economic rationale more than on a social or political principle. Finally, as a wholly political organization the Community of Railways serves as a vehicle for mobilizing and targeting this economic sectors' policy interests. Generally, this means Belgrade-targeted activities, although there are occasionally policies generated on the republic level that require what would in the U.S. system be called "lobbying." The Community was one of three channels for "pressing an interest" identified by the railroad executives. They noted (a) the Federal Institute of Prices, (b) the SPK transportation council, and (c) the Community of Railways. The nature of these options was dealt with in Chapter 3.

An equally impressive actor in the future development of Yugoslavia will be the iron and steel sector of the economy. This heavy industrial portion of the system has been an especially vulnerable and volatile one in the 1960s. It has been besieged by mismanagement, disruption, challenges from light and consumer sectors, and by large scale political interference in part stimulated by the other conditions. The iron and steel industry was establishing its foundation in the "new" Yugoslavia of the 1940s (in an appropriately conservative and Stalinist mold) when change external to the industry began to unsettle, and in some cases undermine, the structure of this heavy industrial sector. The story has not changed much since, though problems seem to have heightened to critical proportions following the reforms of 1965. Most of the leadership of the Iron and Steel Federation is unsettled and outspoken. Strong conservative elements remain which reinforce

TABLE 4

Channels of Interest Articulation

	Via Direct Linkages			Via Intermediary Organizations					
	Federal Assembly	Policy Bureaucracy	Federal Commissions	Industrial Associations and "Communities"	SPK	Republic Economic Chamber	Republican Government	Party	Trade Union

Question: *(A)Would you identify the methods and routes by which you would suggest policy modification (that is, offer advice) to government authorities in Beograd? (B) Are other channels more productive if enterprises feel a dramatic or immediate demand is to be made on the system? Please specify.

	Fed. Assembly	Policy Bureauc.	Fed. Comm.	Ind. Assoc./"Comm."	SPK	Rep. Econ. Chamber	Repub. Govt.	Party	Trade Union
Agriculture and (A)	0	1	4	8	17	16	15	0	1
Light Industry(B) n = 35	0	0	10	13	37	28	22	0	0
Heavy Industry (A) n = 50	0	3	7	7	10	31	22	6	2
(B)	0	1	20	16	9	26	27	1	1
Service Industry(A) n = 21	0	0	14	11	6	2	5	0	0
(B)	0	1	14	8	5	6	6	0	0
Total n = 106	0	6	69	63	84	109	97	7	4
Total "Advice"/"Demands" (A)(B)		4 / 2	25 / 44	26 / 37	33 / 51	49 / 60	42 / 55	6 / 1	3 / 1

*Question: Do "single producers," "key industries," or especially "prominent direktors" have preferred channels for articulating their policy interests? Specify by type.

	Fed. Assembly	Policy Bureauc.	Fed. Comm.	Ind. Assoc./"Comm."	SPK	Rep. Econ. Chamber	Repub. Govt.	Party	Trade Union
Single Producers(A)	2	2	11	0	1	1	2	4	1
(B)	0	1	42	0	2	0	3	3	1
Key Industries (A)	1	2	6	17	18	18	12	2	0
(B)	0	1	36	31	10	10	9	0	0
Prominent (A)	6	17	9	6	21	16	14	3	1
Direktors (B)	9	51	11	6	43	20	14	4	1
Total	18	74	115	60	95	65	54	16	4
Total "Advice"/"Demands" (A)(B)	9 / 9	21 / 53	26 / 89	23 / 37	40 / 55	35 / 30	28 / 26	9 / 7	2 / 2

*Question: Are any of the channels generally more effective or reliable than the others?

	Fed. Assembly	Policy Bureauc.	Fed. Comm.	Ind. Assoc./"Comm."	SPK	Rep. Econ. Chamber	Repub. Govt.	Party	Trade Union
Agriculture and Light Industry	0	0	4	2	4	11	3	0	0
Heavy Industry	0	0	5	3	2	9	1	0	0
Service Industries	0	0	9	3	2	7	0	0	0
Total	0	0	18	8	8	27	4	0	0

*Multiple responses possible.

Source: Compiled by the author.

the tendency of the central government to retain a large measure of control over this group of enterprises. The Iron and Steel Federation is another in the series of extra-governmental industrial associations or "communities." Its membership is also nearly universal, a characteristic shared by these two examples but not a characteristic of all such "communities." It is an especially powerful organization whose emphasis is on the political or policy part of the system. Nonetheless, the sector feels threatened with change, including the easing of government protection and the establishment of market-determined and internationally competitive prices. Its policy efforts are often thwarted in the SPK because most of the SPK membership is made up of steel consuming enterprises who see their interest (economic and otherwise) in conflict with the Iron and Steel Federation. In this situation the Federal Institute of Prices serves as a step-father to the steel producers, shielding them at least temporarily from the assaults of other increasingly powerful sectors, among them tourism and construction.

The Federation is not a new organization, but it is of interest because it has taken on new meaning with the changing nature of both the polity and the economy. As direct government involvement in the management of the economy wanes with the appropriate caveats, politically conservative groups still well represented in some industries, including this one, have recognized an increasing need to press their interests, in this case, in order to retain the political control over the economy. A slightly different way of perceiving this phenomenon is to observe that even the most conservative forces in the system have been forced into playing the game of decentralized and pluralistic politics—the very game they would hope to discredit and abandon. Only a very sharp and thoroughly devastating crisis could tip the scales in their favor. Sources interviewed hint that the Iron and Steel direktors also perceive this and are now striving to cut the pace of change instead of the direction and commitment itself.

Some "communities" are more precisely and rigidly constructed along the lines of a profit-motivated enterprise. One such undertaking is called the "Community of Interests" and is directed from Zagreb. Its program is to search out and provide techniques and equipment for the technological development of primarily agricultural enterprises. At the heart of this organization is a group of innovation-oriented businessmen, some of whom have held political positions and whose careers have been affected by the "rotation principle." As explained to me, this group must (1) turn a profit by establishing a cost for their services, and (2) agree upon a method to divide that profit between the "enterprise partners" (consumers of services) and "common funds" (those specifically assigned to the central group). In 1971 this "Community" had no fewer than ten current projects

59

involving thirty "kombinats" or cooperative enterprises which are
generally agricultural focused. These enterprises are partners in
the support of the Community's services and can opt into its various
programs. Examples of the Community's functions are its "centers."
Currently it runs a computer center, an educational center (for various
levels of management), a development center (new lines of production),
and a marketing center. The Direktor himself portrayed his organization in these words:

> The workers in their enterprises, and the enterprises in
> their industries must pay for all new ideas. Both can buy
> special knowledge. The development service Community
> is always aggressively looking for new projects, new
> directions so that it can continue to serve the enterprises
> as a clearing house for ideas.

From this description it is not adequately clear how very important and central this and other such "communities" have become
to the efficiency, production, and marketing of many Yugoslav enterprises. In most cases, they represent a bridge or a link with techniques which enable the enterprises to develop a competitive position
in the European market, a process which can only point to a quantum
jump in the nature and power of the Yugoslav economy. The need for
reflex policy making (in response to such entrepreneurial thrusts)
is a persistent given for the political elite.
However, this last form of "community" is unlike the others
in the sense that, by virtue of its profit-orientation and its specific
objectives, it has only a peripheral interest in pressing political
demands. In fact, such associations do take an active role especially
on a republic level to mollify any restrictive political policy, but
these business interests are often best served by remaining relatively
invisible to political elites. In early 1972 some of these associations
became the target of serious but as yet not fatal political criticism.
This said, if the cases which this investigation confronted directly
are in any way indicative of such organizations, then it is clear that
the nature of their leadership goes a long way toward insuring a
subtle political voice for the Community's interests. It should be
clear that the Community is a markedly more viable weapon for such
interest articulation than would be any of its parts or an independently
acting enterprise. Some distinct exceptions exist, however, and where
they do, we find a slightly different organizational phenomenon. It is
to this relatively new feature of economic organization that we now
turn.
In the West, one might label it "integration" or the development
of "conglomerates." In Yugoslavia, it is a most interesting and

illustrative development because it is a central characteristic of the rethinking, reformulating, and reorganizing which has come with the political decision to decentralize and the economic thrust toward single unit autonomy. In short, it is a trend which in some ways runs counter to the direction of the economic and political reforms. This too is a dangerously broad generalization because it may imply that such a development was negative and unanticipated. On the contrary, establishment economists rather than politicians seem to acknowledge, as self-evident, that efforts of this kind to "rationalize" the enterprise (basic economic unit) would and did develop. Potential examples abound. However, two convenient cases are examined here—one from the agricultural sector, the other a major manufacturing enterprise.

The agricultural case is drawn from the Slavonia region of Croatia, one of the most productive areas in Yugoslavia. Osijek is the hub of this area, and because a specific case might best be used to illustrate the general matrix of enterprise organization in the region, attention will be focused on Industrijsko-Poljoprivredni Kombinat (IPK; Industrial and Agricultural Combine). The "Kombinat" itself is a creature of organizational consolidation, which in many sections of Yugoslavia takes on the appearance of an agriculturally based conglomerate. The IPK story is a typical one except for the speed and success with which the expansion has taken place. IPK leadership in the person of Ivan Spika as direktor, has facilitated and prodded growth in both new product lines and in foreign as well as domestic marketing. For Spika the keynote to growth and development is "integration." Our discussion fixed on this point to a large measure. IPK is a relatively large Yugoslav kombinat. On some criteria it is the largest in Yugoslavia. After the establishment of the Tito government in Belgrade, Slavonia had approximately 100 enterprises or economic units. Since that time there have been two sharp periods of consolidation or integration. The first, politically motivated, reduced the number of enterprises to nine. The last, since 1965, reduced that number still further to three, the present number. The reasons are diverse, but one looms large: mismanagement. Others of importance were the need (1) to unify as a consumer of common needs, domestic and foreign; (2) to establish a more effective political (that is policy) voice in Belgrade and Zagreb (capital of the republic); and (3) to more effectively market products outside the region or outside Yugoslavia. It should also be mentioned that the comparisons made by workers in a particular region can be a catalyst to integration. When it is clear to them that one enterprise and its leadership have provided greater material returns for the workers' input (labor), then the less successful direktor is vulnerable and will often seek alternatives to his removal by the workers' council. Mergers in the West are often similarly spurred by an uneasy economic situation in one or the other company.

61

IPK has about 9000 workers and its land holdings are extremely impressive. The IPK example is a politically interesting one for many reasons. Superficially, it illustrates the linkage between local politics and the enterprises. In this particular case because IPK is so large it also becomes politically involved in the republic capital on a regular (generally, weekly) basis. Of the 9000 workers approximately 1200 are Party members. One should recall that it has already been suggested that the agricultural sector in general, and this region in particular, is relatively "conservative" politically. Spika is President of the local Party in Osijek and is a member of the Central Committee in Zagreb. When questioned about the Party's role in his enterprise he responded in these ways. Using the integration process as an example, he stated that the Party "nudges" those direktors who resist progress. They can be expelled from the Party and that is a very real and meaningful threat. "The Party leads the enterprises to the proper solution but does not control." He emphasized that decisions in the Party are by secret ballot and all are obligated to accept the outcome. Lest one might draw from this that the now "classic" domination by the Party predicated on political as opposed to economic and social principles is the rule there, let me point out that enterprise direktors hold important if not critical Party positions in the local Party structure. In functional terms this means that the Party is not dominating the enterprises as much as it is a vehicle for the economic elite to retain a weighty voice in local political affairs. This question is clearly one of the "horse and cart" variety. A conclusion which can be drawn from the cases examined in this research, is that while the Party has the power to effectively channel the course of enterprise development, its contemporary disposition is to serve economic growth by very selective involvement, since it is clear that economic growth and stability are the way to social improvement and increased Party strength. As time passes and routines and priorities in the direction of economic primacy are well established, one can speculate that the Party's "power" and position in this overall social environment will be diminished.

This research in Osijek did not reveal a single situation in which the Party tangibly affected IPK policy. The conventional linkages are there, the credibility of the enterprise leadership is well established, the routines for securing Party approval of major decisions (informal more than formal) are adhered to, which in total creates a sense that the progress and growth of the enterprise and the improvement in the worker's life style which results, ultimately contribute to both a theoretical and practical strengthening of all the principals at the local level—Party, direktor, workers, and others.

Spika, whose popularity as direktor can be pinned, in his own words, to "the general progress toward a better life" for the members of his enterprise through consistent growth, appears to be politically visible at the local, regional, and republic levels. If he has a profile at all at the national level it is a very low one. He is represented on the agricultural council in Belgrade while at these other levels he is often personally active. Although Osijek is nearly equidistant between Zagreb and Belgrade, most real political intercourse is with the Croatian capital, Zagreb. The ethnic rationale for this is the easiest, but the economic argument (that developments more commensurate with enterprise goals were ongoing in Zagreb and between Zagreb and foreign firms) is the most convincing. IPK exports large portions of its agriculturally processed and manufactured food products to Italy and to a cross-section of developing countries. It is affiliated with the aforementioned "Community of Interests" in Zagreb and has to its own innovative credit a computer facility, in cooperation with IBM-Vienna, which services not only IPK needs but works on contract for other regional enterprises.

The second example of inter-enterprise consolidation is one of the most dramatic in the manufacturing sector of the Yugoslav economy and certainly the most visible. Yugoslav and Western businessmen alike have heard of Energoinvest's assertive and dynamic course of enterprise development. Like IPK the record of success is largely personalized and symbolized in the person of the direktor, Emerik Blum. Neither Blum nor the enterprise which he directs is typical. Both are extraordinary, yet such vanguard developments in the planning, execution, management, and organization of economic enterprises persist and flourish as a pattern to be emulated in contemporary Yugoslavia. Thus our concern here for the case of this Sarajevo based miniconglomerate.

Founded in 1951 by Blum, then Deputy Minister of the Electrical Industry, a small planning and design enterprise soon grew to a modest 130 worker construction enterprise whose forte was power and heating facilities. Expanding first in allied fields and the product lines necessary for the design and construction functions, Energoinvest in the ensuing two decades has diversified into a full line of electrical equipment and has become a European competitor in the aluminum industry. To the envy of socialist and nonsocialist business executives alike, Energoinvest's performance as an economic unit is impressive. An annual growth in sales of 20 percent since 1951 couples with a 1970 sales record of $66 million, of which half was sold on the foreign markets. The value of the "means of production" (fixed assets) exceed $40 million, one eighth of which is R. & D. Blum himself has projected a 1000 percent increase in sales by the end of the enterprise's current "program" (five year duration). Chronicled throughout the financial world,[3] Blum and Energoinvest have tallied such impressive gains through sound, apt business practice—one critical dimension of which is the organizational pattern of corporate expansion.

The integration, by 1969, of thirty other Yugoslav economic enterprises and operations under the Energoinvest banner is the keynote of growth. Business Week analyzes the Blum magnetism in these terms: "But Blum knew how to sweeten the pot: He promised that wages would always run 10 percent above the national average. He still promises it, with the result requests to sign up with Energoinvest are piled higher than the pen-stand on his desk."[4] Such is the inducement from the workers' perspective. In some ways more tangible is the acquisition of central services—Energoinvest's research and development program, international sales force, and sophisticated top level management—which are otherwise beyond the means of all but the largest enterprises. This, from a management perspective, also "sweetens the pot."

Energoinvest's success has found a catalyst in its early commitment to involvement with foreign business interests and foreign markets. This interaction has taken three principal forms. First, from the beginning Blum emphasized foreign sales as a measure of quality control and competitive standards. Having taken such measures the enterprise was fairly successfully insulated from the negative shock wave of the provisions of the economic reforms which opened Yugoslav production to more open foreign competition. It remains highly aggressive by any sales standards, and has shown itself willing and adept at promoting deals by accepting barter terms.

Second, Blum actively sought the development of joint investment (foreign) with the primary purpose not of securing financing but rather for gaining the technical expertise which often accompanied the business interests of foreign firms. A recent example of the acquisition of technological know-how can be found in an agreement with a Belgian engineering firm to design nuclear energy facilities. Still other cooperative and joint ventures function to establish and secure bases for marketing. Energoinvest enters the 1970s with a number of such relationships, among them Energomex (Mexico) and Energolibija (Libya).

Finally, Energoinvest has set a most interesting precedent by retaining the services of an established management consulting firm from the United States. One interpretation of the significance of this development follows: "Perhaps the surest sign that Energoinvest has arrived, in a corporate sense, is that New York management consultants McKinsey & Co. are currently streamlining Blum's table of organization. 'If the company weren't set up along Western lines,' says McKinsey's Charles Shaw, 'it wouldn't have turned to us to shape them up.'"[5] This research also included interviews with Shaw and his associates assigned to the Energoinvest project.

These cases have meaning to the analyst of Yugoslav politics or comparative politics generally because they are raw examples of

the unsynchronized tones of business and politics. The disharmony
between politically conservative environments, enterprises, and
direktors and aggressive, open, and liberalized business policies
initiated by the direktors, supported by the enterprise workers, and
passively observed by the environment at large, is apparently not
perceived as critical or disruptive. Its short-term contradictions
are glossed over or ignored without any apparent cost to any quarter.
Long-term frictions seem amenable to compromise by the current
Belgrade leadership. To date, the benefactors have been the workers,
whose life styles have improved, even after discounting for the current
wave of inflation. The economy's base is more solid and its momentum
is greater than at any other point in the modern state's development.

Still with the weight of these organizational dimensions of enterprise development, one continues to search for an encompassing
variable which produces the milieu for such decisions in Energoinvest,
IPK, the "Communities of Interest," and so forth. With only a mar-
ginal sense of confiednce that one has thwarted the ethnocentric
impulse to seek out and exalt the leaders of these units and further
to point unceasingly to their pragmatism as the "golden key" to economic success, this investigation now turns to the men of the system
as a source of development and change.

PERSONNEL CHANGE

One distinct direction of change in the contemporary system
is the circulation of the economic elite. Other portions of the Yugoslav elite have also been in flux; however, one would be hard put to
match the scope and importance of personnel changes since 1965 in
any other sector of society or in any period since the Second World
War. It follows that one should be surprised that analysts have, in
general, not taken note of or projected the impact of such a thorough-
going systemic change.[6] From the examination of the literature
prefatory to this study, there appears to be no such treatment. The
preliminary effort which follows is largely descriptive, although some
propositions may be found toward the end of the section that have
comparative significance.

Collectively, elite change can be interpreted in a number of
ways. It may be the precursor of change, the first signal of dislocation
in the system, during which the Establishment purifies and solidifies
its ranks in anticipation of conflict. Or it may be the final signal of
systemic change, the post mortem cleansing of the system by those
whose political authority is newly established and whose program
has triumphed. Evidently a third possibility exists. The advent of
a new elite may not be a function of broad systemic and political

65

change at all. New managerial actors can emerge independent of any factors other than the microsetting in which the immediate circumstances dictated replacement of the incumbents. The recent Yugoslav experience reveals that personnel changes were recorded in significant numbers superficially indicating a collective action in the economic restructuring of the mid-1960s. With this imperfect typology—(a) tactical, (b) resultant, and (c) irrelative change—based on the fundamental relationship of the elite change to the broad flow in the political system, change in the Yugoslav economic elite is examined.

The most evident manner of comparison of the newly established managerial class is through background characteristics: age, education, experience, and political orientation. The universe of data on the full complement of the primarily economic elites in Yugoslavia was beyond the scope of this research. Drawing on that which was obtainable and verifiable, the sample is restricted to enterprise direktors. The total sampled represents about 10 percent of all Yugoslav direktors. The technique of drawing the sample raises some methodological questions about its validity as a qualitatively representative cross-section of the elite. In fact, data was accumulated based on two separate criteria through two sources, for practical as opposed to design purposes. First, the entire listing of biographical portraits was extracted from the Yugoslav direktors professional trade journal, Direktor. Second, direktors were identified through their membership on the central management board of the SPK in Belgrade. In both cases, if one were to anticipate a bias it would be in the direction of the more active, visible professionals in the system. How this appreciably affects the propositions extracted from the data, if it does affect it at all, is unclear to this analyst at the present time. However, the data appear adequate to depict the general character of change among the top economic management.

As noted earlier, those now holding top management positions in Yugoslavia are somewhat younger than one might expect in either a Communist or a developing country. In both, it is characteristic for regimes to strive for a high degree of continuity, especially in a "backbone" elite sector such as the one we are examining. The typical direktor is decisively under fifty years old. The sample revealed a mean age of 45 in 1971. Paralleling this information, he has held the highest position in his firm for seven and one half years (also dated from 1971). Both the youth and the limited longevity of the management group, taken as a whole, would tend to indicate that there is a potential in these men for real innovation, reinforced by the fact that their rise to such important positions as a group came at approximately the same time that national reforms emerged. These constitutional changes fundamentally rededicated the economy to participatory management, leaving the microunits in the economy to make major adjustments in management practice.

Most of the new personnel came up through the firm itself or through enterprises with similar functions or product lines. In essence, few were injected into unfamiliar industries. This contrasts with most managerial change in other communist systems. Vis-à-vis their predecessors, the new elite is better trained in both a "liberal" sense and in the background needed to respond to the leadership needs of the enterprise. Characteristically, the typical direktor has a degree in economics from a Yugoslav faculty, although degrees in law and sociology are also in evidence. Approximately 12 percent of the direktors have no degree at all. While very difficult to represent in any rigorous fashion, an evident contrast emerged in the interviews between those of the "older" and the "younger" generation of direktors. Those closest to the "typical" direktor consistently responded to queries with fewer ideological parables and formulations. Their rather "hard" approach to business matters and criteria of economic efficiency and development are a firm foundation for systemic growth and enterprise regeneration.

The area in which their backgrounds reflect the least overt change is that of political affiliation and experience. Many still have ties with the tail end of the revolutionary struggle. Most of the newer direktors were in their early twenties at the end of the war, and more were to be found in the ranks than in the officer echelons of the Partisans. Their political records are starched with commitment to the Party and nearly all are members of the LCY. Yet only a slight majority consider themselves as being "regularly active" in Party politics and activities.[7] A significant number indicated that pressing enterprise problems keep them from committing "very much" time to Party meetings, activities, and so forth. Two factors seem to affect the degree of Party orientation of enterprise direktors. Size of enterprise and industry are critical variables determining formal political activity. This is particularly true at the local, regional, and republic levels. The relevant propositions are: (1) as the enterprise increases in size (social and financial) the direktor is more likely to be more involved in politics in an overt role; and (2) some industries previously identified as conservative—greater central government control—apparently compel the direktor to remain more visible and active in Party politics. Neither of these are out of line with projection made intuitively by numerous social scientists.

A more subtle political experience can be found among the new group. Older direktors had no opportunity to learn political lessons in the various chambers that exist in the present system. Such exposure has produced greater political sophistication among the new direktors. The longer established executives have little perception of this dimension of enterprise politics, which puts them at a distinct disadvantage politically, vis-à-vis the challenges from younger managers. This situation is ironic in view of the fact that most of the older direktors were responsible for assigning the younger men to their duties in the various chambers. Nearly all direktors in the sample under 50 years of age have had some tangible exposure or experience in one of the political or economic chambers at the district, republic, or national level. In summary, broad changes among direktors in the system have produced a class which better understands the political workings of the system and, in many ways more important, knows what to expect and how to influence the inertia of the system.

The text above suggests that few direktors were injected into managerial positions without having had experience in the firm or the industry. Some exceptions warrant examination and explanation. The "rotation principle"8 affected the job situations of economic elites formerly in elevated positions with chambers or ministries. In essence, most were compelled to step down after a specified term in office. Those left in a precariously "unemployed" category of managers returned to enterprises in their particular areas of expertise while a few of the more entrepreneurial types formed new enterprises. In this latter regard, one of the most interesting developments was the emergence of firms whose function was to service the needs of other enterprises for computer, marketing, and sales expertise, and technological and management consultation. For the economic sector, the application of the rotation principle brought with it not only dislocation, but also a very healthy rethinking of the tangible needs of industry in Yugoslavia. This was largely a function of the individual dilemma of innovative, capable executives turned out of political positions. Their search for new roles in the system proved to be a catalyst to general economic development.

Among the institutions most affected by the "rotation principle" and later by the vast change in enterprise leadership, were the tiers of economic chambers. Men holding executive positions in these organizations at various levels have come to accept as routine the fluidity of their roles and the temporary nature of their positions. The problems of the SPK have been presented at some length in Chapter 3. In spite of continuing difficulties, a vitality and zeal comes to the organization each time a new direktor ascends to the Presidency. This was most clearly the case with the nomination of Rudi Kolak in 1969. Though such enthusiasm may wane, the overpowering consequence of the mandated leadership change is the routinization, institutionalization, and expectation of organizational and policy change in the system. This process has impact on career mobility and counteralienation (political) among the economic elite.

Background characteristics serve as a base for charting the elite changes, but a more subjective analysis may illuminate even more clearly the thrust of the transition. In response to a question put to him by a Dutch analyst, Blum replied: "Measures to promote the efficiency of business-operating have nothing specific to do either with socialism or capitalism. This work can be done either well or badly in both system."9 Business Week reinforces this notion in a recent article on Energoinvest and Blum. "Though the company exists in a nation which does not permit private ownership of industry and where workers' councils have veto rights over management's every move, Yugoslavs do not let these socialist conditions get in the way of productivity and profit."10 This striving for sound business practice, a rigorous approach to economic and enterprise decision-making, dominated the tone and substance of interview sessions. The driving force for improved analytic methods was tempered only by a commitment in principle to the general social well-being of the community. Even these concerns were elaborated upon in terms of their direct implications for enterprise growth and development. At its heart, social commitment is built into and is a function of the economic performance of the enterprise. In serving that end, the direktor also serves the community at large. With the transition of the managerial elite into a group of "professionals," productivity and creativity have increased. One certainly finds, in the most visible firms, direktors who are polished, dynamic, innovative, and effective as corporate heads and representatives of their economic units. "Productivity," "profit," "growth," "incentives," "sales," "marketing," "quality control," and "investment inducement" are an established part of the vocabulary of the contemporary Yugoslav direktor.

As the elite has changed fundamentally, the inertia of the system has been broken. New, younger, better trained, more politically apt, and change oriented men bring a vitality to the system as a whole, increasing its potential if not its performance. This, of course, does not preclude an increased potential for tension and conflict within the system, which at least conceptually may be enhanced.

Finally, this section returns to the basic query with which it began: "Was the mammoth shift in direktor personnel in 1964-65 a tactical, resultant, or irrelative change vis-à-vis the general reform program, already established as a primarily political development?"

The answer is quite clear. Neither the central government, the central Party figures, the "Reformers," nor the "Conservatives" held enough direct control over the managerial elite to effect a thorough-going tactical change. Irrelative change is similarly eliminated because of the substantial numbers involved in personnel changes within a rather narrow span of time. Beyond that, reports reveal that the early and mid-1960s were not especially bad years for most

Yugoslav enterprises. Was there a catalyst, possibly even a causal factor, which precipitated the transformation? The tendency then is to contend that widespread personnel changes were a result of the politically motivated reforms. It is important to note, however, that there is no evidence that the shift in enterprise direktors was manipulated by any political group. Hypothetically, a political faction winning a political battle over the reforms would have had enough power to effect many changes. On the contrary, the pattern of managerial changes would suggest that the reforms served as a psychological and legal opening to those within the enterprise who were aggressively ambitious (and popular) at the microlevel. With the "wave of reform" the stage was set in many firms for a leadership change due to indigenous circumstances within that economic unit. In some sense then, the change was irrelative. Pressures and expectations had mounted in many enterprises which had been met with rather conservative managerial methods and "classic" caution. It is impossible to say conclusively where on the continuum from "catalyst" to "causal factor" the national political and economic reforms lie.

In summary, the substantial leadership change came in step with, not in advance of, the reforms. The new direktors may be contrasted with the old in terms of the type of political experience they have, but their programs and commitments are primarily economic and seldom range beyond the immediate enterprise. They are businessmen aware of their relationship with the political Establishment and cognizant of the channels through which they can press their needs. For most of them politics is a means rather than an end. Apparently their objectives, values, and methods are relatively indistinguishable from their counterparts in many "developed" countries, including the United States.[11] This hypothesis deserves continued investigation beyond the scope of this study.

An effort has been made to establish that organizational developments in the system are intrinsically pragmatic and that elite change is "resultant." Let us now turn to what is often conceptualized as the "cement" of the functioning system: ideology.

IDEOLOGICAL TRANSFORMATION

Ideology has become one of the classic variables in the analysis of developments in all Communist societies. Certainly the reasons are evident, but the result is that some of the least productive writing (polemics) has also been produced on the subject. Any discussion of socialism forces one to return to the Marxian formulation and all the caveats and contradictions implicit in the interpretation and reinterpretation of the most read social scientist in history. It may be folly or it may be begging the question to try to avoid this pitfall, although the subject cannot be dismissed out of hand.

Focusing on the subject of the evolution of the Yugoslav socialist system alone, dozens of eminently qualified scholars have asked and are asking the probing question of the degree and quality of socialism in the Yugoslav experiment.[12] This section proposes to accept as given, that is to say, without a formal proof, that the Yugoslav social experiment is built upon the application of socialist principles to the Yugoslav environment—spatially, temporally, and socially defined. This posited, we can move to the challenge of analyzing the pattern of application and response to the programs of both the central and decentralized bases of authority in the system. The focus, then, will be on what is the essence of ideological tension over the innovations in the system, happily leaving for others the realm of what ought to be the developmental pattern and ideological antagonisms inherent in it.

The ideological progressions experienced by Communist systems in the past twenty-five years illustrate that political and economic change, though fused in doctrine, are actually segments of the social system which do not naturally conform to one another. Beyond this, ideological prescriptions internal to either the "political" or "economic" spheres are less than consistent. The Yugoslav experience reveals an increasing expenditure of effort in the direction of bringing the political and economic realms into a composite form. To accomplish this in a Marxist society the ideological format and the tone of the interpretations put on it must be reworked to the point that an evident contrast emerges between the Soviet and the Yugoslav doctrine. Students of Yugoslav and, more generally, of Communist politics know the costs and dislocation caused by such a fundamental shift. This section will review the course of ideological transformation over recent decades with an eye to highlighting (as opposed to explaining) the essential points of conflict. It will also present a brief analytic sketch of the general and enduring impact which this transformation has had upon the development of the system as a whole.

The doctrinal concepts drawn into focus in this section are: (a) direct democracy, a manifest political doctrine; (b) planning and decentralization, a universal economic doctrine; and (c) workers' self-management, a production level or microeconomic doctrine.[13] These three represent both the substructure of the Marxist-Leninist prescription for the system and the constructive ideological pillars of the new society.

The principal impetus behind the Yugoslav ideological and systemic experimentation was the "reaction against the etatistic and bureaucratic socialism in the Soviet Union."[14] Ideological support for Yugoslav criticisms are to be found in the classic Marxian concepts of the "withering away of the state," the restrained and benevolent role of the Communist Party as representative of proletarian interests, as well as the whole syndrome of other humanist elements. From the Yugoslav perspective much of the Soviet political experience clashed with this guiding doctrine. Drawing particular Yugoslav attention was the Soviet concept of the monolithic, centralized state which manifest itself in "bureaucratism, etatism, full control of ideological trends, especially of cultural creation, that is to say, complete subjugation of the intelligentsia . . . an absolutistic conception of rule 'from above' . . . in the name of the working class."[15]

The Yugoslav ideological argument often returns to a premise offered by Marx himself. He wrote that the proletariat "does not need a social revolution with a political spirit, but a political revolution with a social spirit." Another common point in the running ideological battle with the Soviet Union is the late Bertrand Russell's observation and warning which he offered shortly after the Russian Revolution. Essentially, Russell sensed the possibility that the revolution would be sacrificed to "politics" unless the decisional authority was transferred to workers' councils. He hypothesized that centralization meant that the antagonisms of the proletariat would remain and fester. For Marx, as the state disintegrated man would cease to be alienated from power and instead would be a part of it. His label for this evolving phenomenon was "the free association of producers." The Yugoslav counterpart is "self-governing socialism," which in practice becomes "workers' self-management" at the micro-level. Labels for the kind of socialism implemented by the Yugoslavs range from those noted above to "producers' democracy," "industrial democracy," and "participatory management."

The Yugoslav aversion to Stalinist adjustments of the system was sharp and absolute. A typical indictment follows.

> The fact that Stalin gave a totally different meaning to the dictatorship of the proletariat by rejecting in full the theory of the withering away of the state, and by identifying the social revolution with a complete planification of the economy and with full control of public and cultural life, gave to Soviet socialism that etatist form, which has been criticized so many times before.[16]

Of course, that which remains unsaid is that it was this same Stalinist model which was dominant in the early years of Yugoslav socialist development, and the above statement is therefore implicitly a criticism of that early pattern as well.

As it is now ideologically posited by the indigenous leadership, the basic tension in the system lies in the balancing of "representative democracy" and "self-governing democracy" (direct democracy). This is the juxtaposition of fully decentralized decisional authority and responsibility, and ceded authority and responsibility, presumably centralized in a governmental agent. Political theory and practice on all levels of rule-making and rule-application in the Yugoslav system illustrate the proportions of these two elements. The contemporary system tends to allocate major responsibility to the decentralized elements of the system. Such autonomy is directed though not manipulated, and established itself as peculiar to the socialist system at large and as most efficient and ideologically amenable to the West. This research taken as a whole is committed to the examination of the tangible nature of this realignment of forces in the system as well as charting the implications for broad social development. Chapter 2 examined the juxtaposition of power in the firm or enterprise, Chapter 3 searched for patterns of real policy responsibility between levels in the Federal system in Yugoslavia, and Chapter 5 will review developments and the impetus of foreign economic relations. At each level the ideoolgical underpinning is explicit and visible by design. An example from the previous discussion of the SPK may serve to illustrate this point. At the national level economic decisions are a shared responsibility of the Federal Chamber and the Economic Chamber. The first is ideologically conceived as a "representative" assembly drawing its membership from the society at large, while the second has a "direct" membership in the sense that Chamber personnel are direct agents of the enterprises they represent. The contrast may be subtle, imbedded in the theoretical nature of their roles, or it may be spurious, but the effort to rationalize and typify their roles is clear. On a higher humanistic plane the inherent question is one of "man's right to decide on the essential questions of his own existence."

One of the three conceptual tenets, workers' self-management, functions as the heart of the system. It leads to "the withering of the state" and to the birth of the free association of men. Though universally operative, this concept is in conflict with the need for systemic economic planning and for restrained fiscal control of selected economic sectors. These needs are also rationalized as ideological precepts. Arguments over social and political imperfections of the system are routinely couched in terms of theoretical phases of development. The theoretical dialectics of development are carefully fleshed out by Yugoslav officials. The explicitly political dimension of Yugoslav thought also takes issue with both Soviet and Chinese theories on the need for a single political party with an exclusive claim to political legitimacy. The Yugoslav interpretation provides for a coalition of groups and parties, whose only shared value must be the interest of the proletariat.

73

At the production or microeconomic level the Soviet model prescribes centrally planned control to alleviate spontaneous market forces and the "profiteers' mentality." From this it follows that political power is concentrated in a hierarchy which effectively channels directives downward to the workers. It is this circumstance rather than the motivation which prevents any clearly effective input from below to reach the policy elite. As described by Max Weber, the fusion of economic and political power in the bureaucracy is regarded by many Marxists as the ultimately "rational" production matrix.[17] However, challenges to this view are also commonplace. The most persuasive come from scholars and policy-makers in other socialist systems, among them Ota Sik of Czechoslovakia and E. G. Liberman of the Soviet Union. Other more subtle challenges have been noted in Hungary, Poland, and even in Bulgaria. Doctrinally, the Yugoslavs remain foremost in protesting the pattern of development evident under the classic system. The following criticisms are representative.

> Yugoslav experience has given rise to the following objec-
> tions . . . a certain inability to assess the real possibil-
> ities of the economic development; . . . superfluous admin-
> istrative apparatus at all levels; . . . lack of economic
> initiative or of entrepreneurial dynamism; . . . the ab-
> sence of objective economic criteria in production; . . .
> and inability to link up with the world economy as a
> factor for stimulating and measuring the real produc-
> tivity.[18]

The argument continues that if decentralization is not accepted on its economic merits, it must be understood that the economic system is pressed to adapt to and conform with the political doctrine of direct democracy.

On this dual rationale, a tangible transformation was set in motion. It provided first for an increased role of the workers in managerial functions—increased awareness, participation, and ratification of major enterprise decisions. Systemically, economic growth was enhanced. The principle of "remuneration according to work performed" legitimized incentives with positive results.[19] Light industries were accommodated with provisions for investment, opening "backbone" heavy industries to relatively difficult competitive positions. Change also brought a new, more socially conscious form of the "profiteer mentality," and with it increased attention to a higher standard of living and to income related goals. Inter-firm integration was nurtured to solidify the "rational" production base of the economy. Integration on the initiative of the participants (local units), or to put

74

it another way, integration stimulated from below is propagated on economic reasoning with the additional advantage of modernizing and technologically advancing the economic sector. This is especially the case in Yugoslavia where national differences carry with them many developmental contrasts.

Although one less pressing than the other, another tension derives from the fact that workers' self-management and the relationships which that program engenders, have been created from above, by the government. As a result understanding and enthusiasm for this very basic development is, at best, uneven. In fact, it is such a sharp reversal of management practice (in theory) that resistance to it may still be found in a system which favors the more classic authoritarian structure. As noted in earlier sections of this study, the iron and steel sector is an example.

A final problem threatens traditional Yugoslav ideological premises. Empirical socio-psychological studies, of which there are increasing numbers, point to the advent of technology as a further input necessitating systemic adjustments. Initial studies reveal that business-related problems become more important than organizational or interpersonal problems of workers' self-management. In essence, the workers cease to be alienated as experience in management grows, and this positive concern for enterprise growth puts a strong emphasis on the tangible problems of the firm rather than on the institutional rules of self-management. As one scholar reports:

> This leads us to a general conclusion with regard to the dynamics of a democratic form of managing enterprises: it is always greatest at the beginning, after its introduction, and afterwards slows down gradually, becoming a routine activity, in which the technical problems of running a business predominate over problems of participation of the members and social problems in general. Probably this rule holds good for all newly formed institutions of a democratic character . . . institutions of direct democracy, are subjected to a time dynamics in the sense that participation is greater at the beginning and then becomes more passive, routine, and takes on perhaps a more defensive character.[20]

Beyond this hypothesis, Rudi Supek, a prominent Yugoslav sociologist, assesses:

> when questions are at stake like the economic policy of the enterprise, the relations on the market or relations with other enterprises, the solving of these problems is

generally left to the experts and the proposals by representatives of specialized bodies or of the professional
advisory board of the director, who are not members of
the workers' council, and are generally adopted without
discussion.[21]

There is evidence of the "modification" of ideologically prescribed relationships at the enterprise level in the interview data
presented in Chapter 2. Other studies support these findings.[22]
Drawing on the workers' perception of power in the enterprise, these
investigations suggest an ordinal ranking with the direktor most
powerful, followed by the professional advisory board, the foreman,
the workers' council, and the trade union branch. The same studies
found when seeking the workers' "desired" ranking that the workers'
council was placed first. This latter bit of data must be viewed
cautiously since (1) productive efficiency also ranks high among the
values and priorities of the workers, and (2) workers hold final
responsibility for the shape of management, given their ultimate
authority to dismiss a leadership group with which they are unhappy.
Many cases of the latter have been observed in post-Reform Yugoslavia. In sum, it is clear that today a potential tension derives from
the juxtaposition of power at the local level, a tension which may be
attributed (without normative judgments) to the gap between theory
and practice.
   The democratization of the Yugoslav economy at both micro
and macrolevels is incomplete. Pragmatism is responsible, in part,
as is the modest level of social, educational, and economic development in Yugoslavia. Progress is nonetheless impressive. Ideological
formulations serve the contemporary Yugoslav system as guidelines,
not as cast-iron chains. As such they may be flexible, even malleable.
Finally, a case could certainly be made that the substantial concern
for doctrinal explanations of policy may be principally functional in
a foreign policy sense, vis-à-vis the Soviet Union.
   The ideological transformation of the Yugoslav system is distinct and heuristic. It offers us a proof that the gap between theory
and practice produces numerous systemic tensions. Yet it also
highlights the fact that this conflict can be managed when the priorities of the system lie beyond the purely theoretical. Used as a
theoretical map (a means) rather than an end, ideology seems to
serve many functions in the system: among them integration, communication, legitimization, and socialization.
   The general analysis now turns to the capabilities of the Yugoslav system in an effort to assess the parameters of economic policy-
making.

INDUSTRIAL AND ECONOMIC
SIGNS: CAPABILITY

At this point the variables which provide the <u>currency</u> for policy formation and political efficacy will be examined. The analogy to a financial transaction may be useful. The capability factors dealt with in this analysis serve the politicians and officials (and managers, when politically active) as the symbolic currency or tender, just as currency serves the manager or economic man in his transaction. A political system can be poor or bankrupt in the variables which enable it to act, assess, and respond in a policy sense. Yet in politics as in business, there are skills and finesse which in varying measure can transform minimum potential into disproportionate success. Just as the executive in a firm can pursue business activities through the extension of credit and the "credibility" of his resources, the political executive can develop programs which exceed the apparent limits of his system's capital or, in such a case, its raw capability variables. Clearly this does not invalidate the use of such factors as indicators of systemic strength, nor does it follow that in the real world there are no limits to this kind of speculative policy-making.

It must be reiterated that the variables examined in this section are those which are relevant to domestic and foreign economic conditions and which suggest pervasive influences on the system as a whole. Scholars examining Yugoslav politics principally through descriptive work have consistently concluded that Yugoslavia is a unique system with unique capabilities. The unusual mixture or combination of otherwise recognizable components is responsible for this characterization of the society, polity, and economy of the Yugoslav socialist system. In this model variables presented are fitted as best as possible into a rigorous and system-oriented framework.[23] Domestic and foreign economic policy and their formulation are but one of the policy areas illuminated by the variables chosen. The analysis of economic decision-making is aided by the examination of capability data. Much available data is pertinent and can be meaningfully consumed in a raw form. It is a truism that political decisions about domestic and foreign economic development are a fundamental part of the conduct of the state owing to their impact and "pebble-in-the-pond" effect on the whole system. In this study a preliminary attempt is made to present variables (or types of variables) which affect the tone, nature, and place of economic policy in the over-all political system of Yugoslavia. Considered collectively the variables chosen do suggest a distinct pattern (model) or political and economic development.

Capability has certainly been one of the key traditional concepts used in analyzing policy, whether domestic or foreign—economic or political. Often correlated intuitively with "power," the classical hypothesis holds that capabilities are the independent variable; output (policy) is the dependent variable, and leadership, culture, style, institutions, and process are intervening variables. A further corollary is that the independent and dependent variables are directly related. Thus, the weighting and relationship of these components in the broad conduct of policy formation has remained an unchallenged and untested "given."[24]

Seeking the data necessary to describe the capabilities of Yugoslavia or of any other Communist state is not a routine task. Some reference materials provide basic statistical and quantified measures. Still it is difficult if not impossible to verify such reports by cross-reference. However, the Yugoslav case enables one to rely more heavily on such criteria than does any other Communist society. Two conditions account for this: (1) the eagerness with which the Yugoslavs have participated in United Nations and OECD programs, including information gathering and dissemination, and (2) the Yugoslav Statistical Yearbook (Statisticki Godisnjak Jugoslavije) which is an impressive compilation prepared by the Federal Institute for Statistics, in Belgrade.[25]

For purposes of this examination, "selected capability factors" will be divided into (1) economic base; (2) educational base; (3) political capabilities; (4) "capacity for collective action"; and (5) international environment.

Economic Base. Materially, indicators of arable land, energy resources, and raw mineral wealth are readily available. The Yugoslav state reports that there are 10.2 million hectares under cultivation with a population per square mile of arable land of approximately 600. Essentially this reflects the relatively high ratio (for Eastern Europe) of population to productive land which is a consequence of Yugoslavia's varied landforms and of a large, naturally forested countryside. Energy production (hydroelectric) is moderately impressive with 19 billion kilowatt hours being produced annually which supply the Yugoslav consumer with an average of 753 KWH per year. Generally assessed, basic raw materials exist in quantities abundant enough to have kept pace with domestic industrial demands. Of variables focusing on the state's economic condition, most analyses accept the proposition from Rudolph Rummel's "Dimensionality of Nations" project research that most descriptive economic indicators are strongly correlated to GNP-related measures. Thus, in an effort to avoid a shotgun approach to representing economic power, a few of those GNP-associated variables of particular interest are presented in the data column of Table 5. Annual revenue and expenditure figures also appear there. However, one economic aspect of the

78

TABLE 5

Capability Data

Area (square miles)	98,700	GNP (1957)*	4,779
Population thousands (1967)	20,000	GNP (1975)projected)*	20,089
		GNP per capita* (1957)	265
Population projection (1975)	21,686	GNP per capita* (1975)	926
Population per square mi. arable land (1967)	600	GNP—percent annual average change* (1953-60)	7.2
Million hectares cultivated (1967)	10.2	GNP—percent annual average change* (1957-75)	11.0+
Percent employed in industry (1966)	18.5	Per capita average annual income* (1967)	325
Percent labor force in agriculture (1975)	56.0	Nat'l revenue* (1967)	1505
Percent total area cultivated	40.0	Balance of payments* (1965)	+23.3
Number institutions of higher learning (1967)	260	(1966)	-69.2
		(1967)	-119.2
Percent literate (15 years and over) (1967)	76	Steel produced (1967) metric tons	1,832,000
Speakers of domestic languages as percent of population (1953)	73.2	Deaths from domestic group violence (1950-62)	0
Percent literate—15 and over (1975 proj.)	87.5	Radios per thousand population (1967)	120
Annual per capita consumption of electricity in kwh	753	Radios per thousand (1975)	188.2
Electric energy produced million kwh	18,702	Executive Stability Index (1945-70)	25.0
Military personnel as percent of total population (1959)	2.17	Telephones per 1000 (1967)	19.0
Military personnel as percent of total population (1967)	1.35	Number of countries with diplomatic relations	90
Men in armed forces	270,000		
Expenditure on defense as percent of GNP (1959)	7.30		

*Millions of dollars.

Yugoslav system can elude the analyst in the thicket of mathematical and econometric indicators. Reference is made here to the level of development (or social development) of the industrial, commercial, financial, and trade sectors of the decentralized Yugoslav enterprise system. The collective leadership and direction of the managerial elite working in a semi-independent environment have stimulated a growth and development which significantly complement the political leadership's pursuits. This growth itself is a factor in the capability of the system and in the confidence it inspires.

The World Outlook 1970 (a reputable product of The Economist's intelligence unit) summarizes the dominant, current features of the Yugoslav economy.

> Although it is expected that the very high growth rate in the economy will slow down towards the end of next year, . . . consumption will continue to run ahead of production. Consequently, inflation is certain to continue. The trade gap is likely to widen but the effects of this will have been mitigated by a record inflow from tourism, and by renewed efforts to get Yugoslavs working abroad to repatriate their foreign earnings. The inflow of foreign capital will increase as a result of the foundation of the International Investment Corporation for Yugoslavia, but . . . until further inducements are created and confidence in the economy built up, the benefits to Yugoslavia will be slow to develop.[26]

One can see in this assessment programs which are both uncommon and unprecedented in a Communist state, as well as a distinct external or outward looking orientation of the economy. Drawing from the analysis in Chapters 2, 3, and earlier sections of this chapter, it is hypothesized that the Yugoslav managerial elite, working with (but not for) the political elite, is responsible for the two developments cited above. External orientation will be discussed explicitly later as a critical input into the development of the state's economic system.

Educational Base. Population figures found in the capability tables indicate both raw size and projected growth by 1975. Ethnic homogeneity is reflected in the variable labelled "Speakers of dominant language as percentage of population." 73.2 percent of those living in the Yugoslav state spoke Serbo-Croatian (1953). This is relatively low (lowest of percentages for any Communist state) and is reinforced by the multiplicity of nationalities indicating the degree of heterogeneity. Cultural and educational levels are indicated by a set of variables which include percentage of population literate, number of institutions of higher learning, and number of school pupils as a percentage of the population segment between five and nineteen years of age. Although Yugoslavia registers only moderate levels in the first and last of these categories, it is second only to the Soviet Union in institutions, enrollments, and graduates of higher education. While of utmost interest, the distribution of technical and organizational skills remains one of those elusive measures which will have to be deferred for future investigations.

Political Capabilities. In terms of political capabilities narrowly defined, two factors are included. First is the degree of government commitment, in personnel and revenue, to economic issues both foreign and domestic, and second, the penetration of foreign interests (control) into the domestic political system. The amount of resources dedicated to the economic sector clearly illustrates the preponderant political concern with economic progress and related matters. Evidence of this commitment of energies is clear whether one is focusing on manpower, research, or the demand and supply of published materials. (A discussion of these materials may be found at the end of this section.)

Yugoslavia currently has diplomatic relations with ninety countries; of these seventy-five are full-status ambassadorial relations. Economic sections and special missions are a priority for Yugoslav foreign service establishments. This represents an official set of external political and economic linkages which, in the Communist world, is second only to that of the Soviet Union, and which provides impressive informational and communicative resources.

The degree of foreign political penetration into the domestic political affairs of Yugoslavia is negligible. However, although diminishing in size as a result of pointed assaults by the Tito forces, it is clear that a group does exist within the LCY which might be characterized as "conservative and Stalinist." Given thrusts of moderation and compromise in the Party coupled with auspicious purges, it is likely that those who remain in the system have so compromised themselves that their collective manifest political effect is nil. Their latent political potential is a subject about which speculation is very difficult. Consequently, in discussion of contemporary Yugoslav politics it is untenable to suggest that any foreign power has significant political influence over the affairs of state or over any group which might influence such affairs.

Capacity for Collective Action. "Capacity for Collective Action" is a label borrowed from David Wilkinson to whom the partial working definition can be credited. Under this heading are subsumed social, psychological, and political facets. In search for meaningful reflections of the social matrix into which "degree of social integration, cohesion, unity, discipline, and organization"27 can be put, an investigator is hard pressed to find a single variable with a strong correlation to this set of conceptual factors. One is forced to respond with an equally disjointed set of variables which are basically stability and communication focused. If one is to accept the validity of these variables vis-à-vis social integration and so forth, it will be necessary to accept that intra-social communication promotes, that is, is positively related to, organization and integration, and that stability engenders unity and solidarity if not consent. These propositions probably deserve much closer independent examination, but for the moment we shall make use of them. When we attempt to use stability as an indicator of social discipline and institutional flexibility, we are, it seems, on much firmer ground.

There are an average of 120 radios per thousand Yugoslavs, and in 1975 that number is expected to be raised by over 50 percent to 188.2. In 1967 there were 19 telephones per thousand population. In this respect Yugoslavia does not compare favorably with other contemporary Communist states. However, on measures of stability selected for this study Yugoslavia far exceeds the other states. Two less than satisfying measures are used: an "Executive Stability Index" computed by dividing number of years independent (since World War II) by the number of heads of state who have held power, and total deaths from domestic group violence. Other variables including a more in-depth examination of political elite change may be found in the research and writing of R. Barry Farrell, Carl Beck, William Bishop, and others. At the intermediate levels of Party and national positions, change is much more readily apparent. The salient feature, however, may be that continuity was preserved from the top. Leadership stability in the economic sector reflects a rather more fluid pattern (see this Chapter, "Personnel Change"). On the former variable, that is, the index, the Yugoslav state shows a perfect, maximum score (25.0) as a function of Josaf Broz Tito's "permanent residency." On the latter, total deaths from domestic group violence (1950-62), a figure of zero was reported. Therefore, if these are minimally adequate variables bearing the hypothesized relationship to discipline and flexibility, on the one hand, and cohesion, solidarity, and "popular unity," on the other, our finding is in line with the intuitively apparent political and personal popularity of the Yugoslav leader, and secondarily, of the system he has molded.

Moral or psychological factors can be divided into two sets: (a) morale, spirit, and perseverance; (b) inventiveness, flexibility, and adaptability. "National character" is a meaningful term only when carefully defined to include all of these and other concepts.

Subjective evaluations are inherently disturbing and justifiably vulnerable. Yet one cannot ignore the moral and psychological complexion of the society. Clearly, the observations which follow are of a highly tentative nature. With reference to the first set (morale, spirit, and perseverance), the Yugoslavs could probably hold their own if some measure of cross-national comparison were available. National and ethnic identifications within the state reflecting sometimes sharp cultural diversity could be used to call this proposition into question. This diversity thwarts efforts to make generalizations about the characteristics comprising the second set. An inclusive and empirical assessment of Yugoslav inventiveness, flexibility, and adaptability would probably paint a very dim picture indeed. Exceptions exist. Slovenes, some Croats, and fewer Serbs have personified many of these qualities as measured by occupational performance. Given the traditions and routines of the past, some are remarkably adaptable and innovative. On balance, one would be challenged to produce a measure or index which could be used to compare Yugoslavia favorably in these respects with most other Eastern European states.

International Environment. Of particular relevance to Yugoslavia's international environment are three spatial factors: facility of access to external areas, factors pertaining to neighboring states, and distance from area-dominant super-power. Yugoslavia enjoys the most accessible geographic location in Eastern Europe. Three of its neighbors are noncommunist states while four others are Communist party states. It is at no point contiguous with the Soviet Union. Three of the four Communist states are Warsaw Pact members while two of the three non-Communist neighbors are NATO members. However, none of these five are "central" states (in a power sense) in their respective alliances. In all, Yugoslavia holds a relatively positive and enviable geographic position which affords both access and a measure of political insulation.

The military posture and emphasis of the state constitute a response to the environment, which in turn is itself a capability factor. Total defense expenditure as a percentage of GNP, the number of men in the armed forces as a percentage of total population, and some notion of the dependence of the state on the supply of arms from external sources seem adequate to represent the military factor in Yugoslav policy formulation. The Institute for Strategic Studies in London is a valuable source of data on this dimension of Yugoslav capabilities. Military personnel as a percentage of total population has decreased from 2.17 percent in 1959 to 1.35 percent in 1967. In 1970 there were just under 300,000 men in the Yugoslav armed services most of whom have a one year commitment. Defense expenditure as a percentage of GNP was 7.3 percent in 1959 and, in

TABLE 6

Yugoslav Capability Data: Trade and Balance of Payments
(Selected Imports-Exports for 6 month period January-June 1969 in United States $[a])

Total Imports/Exports to Communist States	Imports	Exports
World	1,036,917,000	641,234,000
With Communist States[b]	254,139,000	190,824,000
Electrical Energy	908,000	54,000
Electrical Energy, with Communist States	730,000	none
Iron and Steel	71,045, 000	19,327,000
Iron and Steel, with Communist States	29,781,000	9,550,000
Firearms of War and ammunition	10,000	none
Firearms of War and ammunition with Communist States	none	none
By country, in U.S. dollars.		
USSR	87,417,000	92,367,000
East Germany	38,931,000	17,408,000
Poland	24,417,000	19,559,000
Czechoslovakia	60,919,000	22,918,000
Hungary	20,178,000	19,147,000
Romania	11,269,000	8,787,000
Bulgaria	9,660,000	9,050,000
Albania	745,000	1,266,000
China	603,000	314,000
North Korea	—	—
North Vietnam	—	—

[a]Yearly projections may be attained by doubling figures.

[b]"Communist States" include USSR, East Germany, Poland, Czechoslovakia, Hungary, Romania, Bulgaria, Albania, China, North Korea, North Vietnam.

Source: OECD Statistics of Foreign Trade, Series C Trade by Commodities, Jan.-June 1969.

spite of the lack of more recent data, this percentage has probably gone up significantly during the late-1960s. Yugoslavia is currently using weapon systems and equipment produced by no less than five different nations. It is also worthy of note that the Yugoslavs are making a concerted effort to manufacture their own military equipment, especially in the areas of tactical and training aircraft, including helicopters. During the first six months of 1969 the government purchased "Firearms of war and ammunition" valued at approximately $10,000 entirely from non-Communist nations (Table 6). Since the thoroughgoing economic and social reforms of 1965, some groups have actively pressured for a decentralized military establishment with independent regional commands. The federal government has to date effectively avoided the issue.

Quantification of the capability variables for any single state is of little value to the comparative analyst without some parallel data on the states within the same international subsystem or within some other general frame of reference. An effort in this direction is made in a forthcoming volume, J. A. Kuhlman and R. P. Farkas, Communist State Systems: A Comparative Approach.

For heuristic purposes one might find it useful to settle on a single value, an index, for a state's capability.[28] From this index a ranking within the frame of reference (system) would be possible which in turn could be compared with (and conceivably challenge) rankings more classically devised.

This discussion of capabilities is meant to represent schematically the politically relevant "capability" of Yugoslavia. Measures of Yugoslav national capability, analyzed comparatively, can serve as a firm base from which to examine the system's economic and political behavior.

RECORD OF PUBLISHING AS A MEASURE OF SYSTEMIC DIRECTION

Another sign of industrial and economic commitment in the Yugoslav system and a variable of interesting proportions is the production and orientation of the publishing field. Developments in the publishing industry in Yugoslavia serve to reinforce many tentative conclusions reached in earlier sections of this research.

Official statistical analysts in Yugoslavia differentiate between publications of the following types: "political," "economic," and "applied economics and business organization." This differentaition implies an astute delineation between economic theory and practice in the business community which no other Eastern European communist state has acknowledged. The real significance is deeper.

TABLE 7

Yugoslav Capability Summary

	Variable Sets	Comment	Relative Assessment
1.	Facility for access to external areas Factors pertaining to neighboring states Distance from area dominant super-power	Accessible to neighbors, distance from Soviet Union relatively great, politically insulated	High
2.	Arable land Energy resources Raw mineral wealth	High population to arable land	Low–Moderate
3.	Ethnic homogeneity		Low
4.	Percentage of population literate Number of institutions of higher education School pupils as percentage of population (5–19)	Second to Soviet Union	Moderate–High
5.	GNP-related measures	High projected increase	Low
6.	Total defense expenditure as percent of GNP Number men in armed forces as percent of total population Dependence on foreign states for military supply	Increasing decreasing buys from 5 states	Moderate
7.	Degree of government commitment to foreign representation Foreign penetration (political)		High
8.	Capacity for collective action: Communications		Low
9.	Capacity for collective action: Stability		tenuously High
10.	Morale, spirit, perseverance	Sharp national diversity	Moderate
11.	Inventiveness, flexibility, adaptability	Not productivity oriented	Low

Source: Compiled by the author.

The charts point to the timing, growth, and juxtaposition of the system's publishing priorities and possibly even to its consumption. We shall begin with the assumption (which is not critical) that there is a positive correlation between the publishing of materials and the consumptive needs of the system. As a corollary, the general pattern of publishing also reflects a measure of control—restraint and sponsorship—by the central authorities. If these propositions are valid, and there is much to suggest they are, then the significance of this dimension is enhanced.

The data is drawn from the mid-1960s, now established as a critical period for the development of Yugoslavia in terms of change and redirection. The flux is evident on the charts. Charts A, C, and D indicate that before 1964 publications of an "applied" nature were relatively less available. Note as well that in 1963 more titles of this sort were translated into Serbo-Croatian than from either the political or economic categories. Reaching a climax in 1966, the number of translated titles and [read-foreign] total titles, shows a steady increase. An examination of Chart B vis-à-vis Chart D reveals that while the number of translated "applied" titles declined in 1967 the number of copies printed multiplied sixfold. Clearly the promotion and consumption of management studies had reached a very high point. Although not surprising if earlier observations about the economic elite in this manuscript are accurate, by 1968 the number of translated titles and translated copies declined sharply, but the number of "total titles" and "total copies" rose inversely. This points to the tangible development of research, reflections, and writing by indigenous Yugoslav analysts on the applied problems and conditions of economic and enterprise development. There is a wealth of indicators which suggest that this is continuing in an impressive fashion to this time. One should be cautioned that this does not mean that Yugoslavs are turning inward for their informational and theoretical guidelines for management. As indicated elsewhere in this paper, there is much evidence proving that Yugoslavs look outward. They are, however, looking increasingly to their own scholars for an empirical portrait of the tangible aspects of the system. This illustrates the evolution of an analytic capability and dedication within Yugoslavia to the subject area of applied economics and business organization.

These findings add credence to an earlier hypothesis (see above, p. 70) regarding the nature of elite change (direktors) in the economic sector. According to that hypothesis, the change was largely "resultant," meaning that it was not manipulated by the political system. "Irrelative" change was also eliminated; change altogether disassociated from the reforms at the national level. The major thrust of personnel change came in 1964-65 and vitality in the publishing area followed in 1966-68. That the "push" in production and consumption of materials emerged only after the clientele had

TABLE 8

Volume of Publishing—Selected Subject Areas

Year	Total Titles			Translated Titles			Total Copies (thousands)			Translated Copies (thousands)		
	Economic	Applied Economics and Business Organization	Political	Economic	Applied Economics and Business Organization	Political	Economic	Applied Economics and Business Organization	Political	Economic	Applied Economics and Business Organization	Political
1963	418	324	245	2	7	3	1403	1498	1795	4	30	41
1964	701	432	383	6	6	1	2364	2326	2301	9	17	1
1965	531	503	423	8	15	4	1669	2680	1990	17	29	31
1966	482	685	327	11	17	11	1579	2550	1964	33	35	26
1967	764	537	320	10	14	12	2030	2581	1679	23	183	45
1968	731	754	325	10	10	15	2282	4269	1844	47	71	143

Source: Yugoslav Survey, November 1969, Statisticki Godisnjak Jugoslavije 1969, and Yugoslav Facts & Views, March 5, 1970.

88

FIGURE 3

Volume of Publishing

(A)

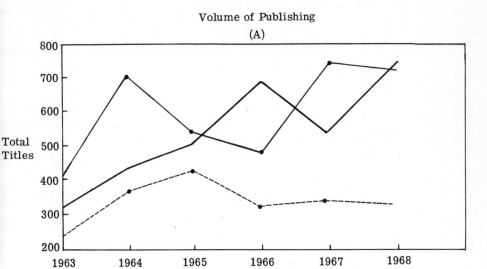

(B)

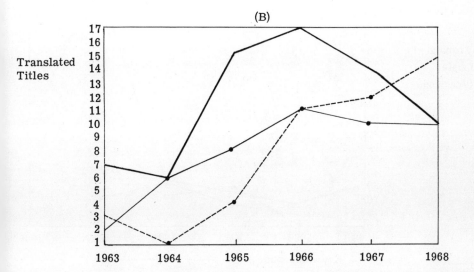

FIGURE 3 continued

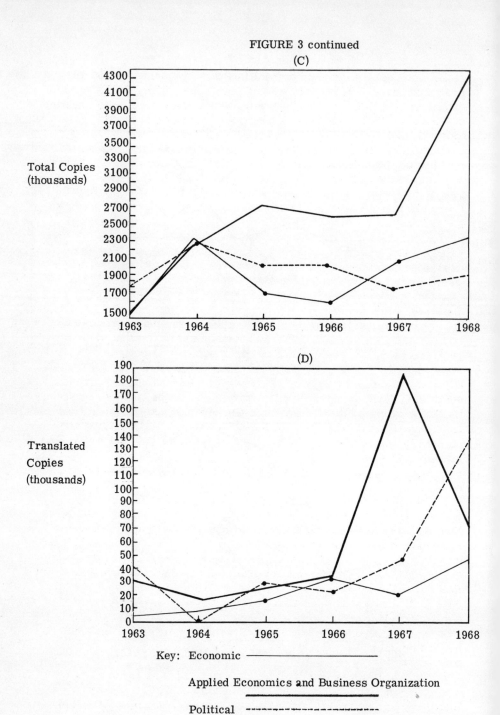

(C)

Total Copies (thousands)

(D)

Translated Copies (thousands)

Key: Economic ————————————

Applied Economics and Business Organization
————————————

Political ------------------------------

90

established itself is further proof of the lack of a system-wide, pro-
grammed change. When such a startling shift in publishing patterns
did take place in the ensuing years (without a more substantial passage
of time), the argument that those personnel changes were not coin-
cidental, isolated instances of intra-enterprise maneuvering is
strengthened. The fact that they were associated but not manipulated
by national reforms is clear.

Some attention must now be focused on the meaning of the publishing data with regard to the relationships between the "applied"
literature and the other two categories—pure economics and politics.

Focusing on the political literature, we find that the levels of
publishing are consistently lower than in the case of the "applied"
category and generally though irregularly comparable to the works
in pure economics. In 1968 (the most recent figures), political titles
(total) were 4 percent of either of the other two categories. From
Chart C, it may be noted that in 1968 approximately 1.85 million
copies of political titles were produced while economics had 2.3
million copies and the AEBO (Applied Economics and Business Organization) category had 4.27 million copies published. In that same
year, however, political publishing significantly out-distanced the
other classifications under both "translated" headings—Charts B and
D. A staisfactory explanation of this phenomenon would be very
desirable. None is readily evident to this analyst beyond the possibility that growing political reaction to the new emphasis of the system
brought a renewal of political dialogue. Unfortunately this does not
account for the fact that the increase is to be found only in the "translated" categories.

The tentative conclusion to be drawn is that there is little or
no pattern, no evident correlation between the thrusts of publishing
of "applied" literature (translated or domestic) with either or all of
the other categories. This alone may be significant. It may also be
that the production and consumption of managerial studies and materials did not follow hand-in-hand with the dynamics of either political
or pure economic thinking. This proposition must be seriously
qualified by the degree to which we can infer a general truth from
this limited data. Of greater importance is its contribution to the
case built throughout: that managerial innovation—psychological,
social, organizational, economic, and political—is a fundamentally
independent phenomenon in the sense that it is neither controlled
nor manipulated nor sterile. It is momentum-bearing and produces
its own ideology.

A final observation about the data on publishing is necessary.
The reporting, acknowledgment, and analysis as well as the raw
magnitude of the "translated" category (that is, foreign scholarship)
is ample justification for emphasizing Yugoslavia's openness and

TABLE 9

Years of Matching Slopes
(pos-pos or neg-neg)

Chart	AEBO/Economic	AEBO/Politics	Economic/Politics	AEBO/Economic/Politics
A	1963-64	1963-64 1964-65	1963-64 1965-66 1966-67 1967-68	1963-64
B	1964-65 1965-66 1966-67 1967-68	1963-64 1964-65 1965-66	1964-65 1965-66 1966-67	1964-65 1965-66
C	1963-64 1965-66 1966-67 1967-68	1963-64 1965-66 1967-68	1963-64 1964-65 1965-66 1967-68	1963-64 1965-66 1967-68
D	1964-65 1965-66	1963-64 1964-65 1966-67	1964-65 1967-68	1964-65
	11-20	11-20	13-20	7-20

Source: Compiled by author.

sophisticated regard for the contribution foreign scholar/analysts can make to her domestic development. This external orientation so readily identified in many aspects of Yugoslav systemic and sub-systemic behavior is considered in Chapter 5.

Basic organization, personnel, and ideological change have created a milieu in which all levels of Yugoslav economic decision-makers can seize opportunities for economic contacts in the foreign market. A review of these contacts, their magnitude and substance, is presented in Chapter 5 in the context of establishing the balance and dependence between foreign and domestic economic activity.

NOTES

1. Jasha Almuli, "Good Future for Joint Ventures," The Financial Times, April 1971, p. 15.

2. Ibid.

3. Among many references, two recent citations from leading American business periodicals are: "A Socialist Conglomerate Builds Up Steam," Business Week, February 14, 1970, pp. 118-20; Gilbert Burck, "A Socialist Enterprise That Acts Like A Fierce Capitalist Competitor," Fortune, January 1972, pp. 82-86ff.

4. "A Socialist Conglomerate Builds Up Steam," Business Week, p. 118.

5. Ibid.

6. The literature represented in the bibliography is devoid of any discussion of patterns of elite change in the economic sector. One exception is: S. Grozdanic, "Administrative Management of Public Enterprises in Yugoslavia," International Review of Administrative Sciences, 32, 1966, pp. 43-57.

7. The suggested criteria for "regular activity" were evidence of any one or combination of the following: (1) routine attendance and participation in Party meetings; (2) a commitment to a formal role or office in the Party; (3) a propensity to give priority to Party affairs; and (4) formal or informal consultation with Party officials on a weekly or monthly basis.

8. Practice and Theory of Socialist Development In Yugoslavia, pp. 148-151, 226-232.

The introduction of the rotation system and the limited re-election principle also marks a significant step forward in the democratization of our cadre policy. . . . One of the most important aspects of the rotation principle is that it contributes to the transfer of public appointments and numerous other posts from a limited number of people to a large number of new ones. . . . We must continue to crush the erroneous bureaucratic belief that the worth of Communists and public official[s] is to be measured in terms of the number of offices [they hold] in government service and social organizations. We must fight, and fight to the finish, to secure esteem and public prestige for every office, and for the holder of that office in accordance with his real worth. . . . It has been shown in practice that to keep cadres at the same duties for a long time tends, apart from other shortcomings, to produce an unimaginative official in the League of Communists, in the organizations of the economy, in the trade unions, and elsewhere. . . . Provision has been made for at least one quarter of the existing leadership to be replaced at each election.

Though the precise period and controls on rotation vary through the system, the concept of elite rotation is very firmly established.

9. M. J. Broekmeyer (ed), Yugoslav Workers' Self-Management, D. Reidel Publishing Company, Dordrecht, Holland, 1970, p. 210.

10. "A Socialist Conglomerate Builds Up Steam," Business Week, p. 118.

11. Though no rigorous data is available to cite as proof of this proposition, interviews with Western businessmen have suggested that this is at least the dominant perception among those most directly in contact with their opposite numbers in Yugoslavia. The similarity of language and ease with which objectives and methods are discussed lend credibility to this sharing of patterns of thought and behavior.

12. Deborah Milenkovitch, Egon Neuberger, Edward Kardelj, and others have discussed this issue from an economic perspective, but a more challenging discussion may be found in the more recent writing of M. George Zaninovich including "The Yugoslav Variation on Marx," in W. Vucinich (ed.), Contemporary Yugoslavia: Twenty Years of Socialist Experiment, University of California Press, Berkeley, 1969; and M. G. Zaninovich, The Development of Socialist Yugoslavia, John Hopkins Press, Baltimore, 1968. Praxis and Socialist Thought and Practice are indigenous sources which also dedicate a substantial measure of concern to this substantive area.

13. Rudi Supek, "Problems and Perspectives of Workers' Selfmanagement in Yugoslavia," in Broekmeyer op. cit., p. 216.

14. Ibid., p. 217.

15. Ibid.

16. Ibid., p. 219.

17. Weber's view is endorsed by Baran, Bettelheim, Sweezy, and other prominent European Marxists.

18. Supek, loc. cit., p. 224. See also Branko Horvat, Essay on Yugoslav Society, New York, 1969, for a full review of criticisms.

19. Institutional restraints limit the wage-differential to 1:3 (lowest to highest) in educational fields; 1:5 in most economic fields. A few professions are less directly controlled including finance, medicine, tourism, and services.

20. Supek, loc. cit., p. 231.

21. Ibid.

22. E. Pusic, Selfmanagement, Narodne Novine, Zagreb, 1968; Workers' Selfmanagement in Theory and Practice, Institut Drustvenih Nauka, Belgrade, 1964; Z. Tanic, "Some Tendencies in the Workers' Councils So Far," Sociologija, Vol. 2, 1961; R. Supek and J. Obradovic, Studies, Institut za Drustevena Istrazivanja, Zagreb, 1968-70; J. Zupanov, "Some Empirical Data on the Responsibility in Working Organizations," Organizacija in kadrovska politika, Vol. 3/4, 1967; The Director under Conditions of Selfmanagement, Ekonomski Institut, Zagreb, 1967; and Kavcic, Rus, and Tannelbaum, "Participation and Effectiveness in Four Yugoslav Industrial Organizations," Ljubljana, 1968.

23. David Wilkinson, Comparative Foreign Relations: Framework and Methods, Dickenson Publishing Co., Belmont, California, 1969.

24. A complete discussion of this premise may be found in R. Farkas, "Contemporary Yugoslav Foreign Policy," in J. Kuhlman (ed.), The Foreign Policies of Eastern Europe: Domestic and International Determinants, forthcoming.

25. All of the chosen variables do not lend themselves to quantification and others remain difficult to code. As these problems are confronted, a subjective evaluation of the capability level has been made. Such "soft" assessments are temporary concessions to the difficulties at hand. Future efforts can speak to the problem of reconceptualizing, sophisticating, or replacing such stubborn variables. The concept of capability hardly requires precise operationalization; however, the dimensions selected for analysis in this study might. In some instances the categories are imperfect and force an altogether too arbitrary placement of specific variables. While this is of concern, it is hardly cause for alarm if it is acknowledged that each is an integrated component (characteristic) of a functionally whole system.

26. World Outlook 1970, Economist Intelligence Unit, Spencer House, London, 1970, p. 33.

27. Wilkinson, op. cit., p. 34.

28. An index of this type is discussed in an unpublished paper by this researcher presented to the Southern AAASS, November 1970, entitled: "Yugoslav Foreign Policy—A Capability Analysis."

5

**FOREIGN
ECONOMIC RELATIONS**

In this chapter propositions will be offered on the subjects of the magnitude, features, and developmental pattern of Yugoslavia's foreign economic relations. The fusion of foreign and domestic economic and political developments makes this a challenging analytic task. The available scholarship testifies that both realms are complex, multifaceted dimensions of the social system. However, this research would hardly be complete had it neglected this "level" of systemic behavior.

The international environment has put parameters on the manner in which "developing" countries can seek to (a) sustain domestic growth and (b) nurture stability. Mid-twentieth-century factors including the nature of the bipolar or tripolar world, messianic ideologies, the club-like control of international economics, and the more subtle rewards system have collectively forced states to be dependent on the pursuit of external relations. With this as a given, and with the peculiar Yugoslav needs augmenting such a trend, a clear case can be built that the relationship between domestic and foreign economic policy is indeed a very strong one. It follows that foreign economic policy holds a central role in the general development of the social system and that it does this as a function of a mutually reinforcing set of factors. The political establishment and its critics are profoundly aware of the implications of the success and failure of external policy and, in this way, such matters have become acute policy-relevant considerations.

Evidence of this importance, especially to the subjects receiving priority in earlier chapters, will be presented throughout this chapter. Two specific tasks are undertaken here. First, it is designed to illustrate the principal programs and directions of Yugoslav international behavior, reflecting the goals, priorities, and techniques of the system. Second, this chapter may serve to reinforce propositions offered in the earlier, domestically-focused analyses. In this way, it may integrate ideas from the domestic and international dimensions of the system, and may also provide still other examples of the flexibility, decentralization, and autonomy of subsystems.

This chapter is organized into three parts: first, a brief and general discussion of the guidelines of Yugoslav foreign policy; second, an examination of the importance and rationale of foreign economic relations; and third, an analysis of the meaningful implications of this contemporary thrust of Yugoslav activity.

GENERAL GUIDELINES OF FOREIGN POLICY

The general guidelines of Yugoslav international policy are susceptible to interpretations from many perspectives. In other research the subject has been analyzed in these terms: "Foreign policy in the Seventies has been and will be developed and executed along five substantive central themes:

1. 'Non-alignment'
2. United Nations oriented policies (including supplementary international organizations)
3. Role in the Communist system (heretic, model, or whatever)
4. Foreign policy specifically contributing to domestic political development
5. Foreign policy of the economic sector (including EEC, EFTA)."[1]

Because foreign economic policy is identified separately and specifically, the meshing or interdependence of these directions of policy may be obscured. By forfeiting a modest degree of control over foreign relations of an economic nature (decentralization), the system has reduced its ability to carefully manipulate the threads of policy. This means that while the threads are still woven into a single cloth, the final design is no longer easily planned or anticipated. The "economic interest" is clearly not the dominant input in all five of the above themes. Yet the economic aspect of each can be identified. Indeed, it may be hypothesized that it is this preoccupation with the economic needs of the system that forges a minimum harmony among the five. A relevant observation is made by the study cited above:

> The sharpest problems and most volatile political challenges will come when these lines of policy tangle. When a friction develops between any two or more of these "modern tradition" policy themes, the Yugoslav system seems susceptible to a polarization along any number of issue or group defined lines. This could

generate the single greatest danger to the contemporary
direction of Yugoslav foreign policy and in turn to the
further development of economic interests: the polariza-
tion of groups ("prescriptive" vs. "will" leadership groups
or economic vs. political foreign policy interests). In either
case, the result, the internalization of Yugoslav foreign
policy, could become a challenge of major proportions
to the political system not without reverberating conse-
quences for all of Eastern Europe.[2]

The latent conflicts alluded to in the above passage do not significantly
detract from a very credible record of successes in foreign relations.
Yugoslav foreign policy has a high degree of flexibility by any standard and is marked by a fine balance between ideological and pragmatic guidelines. "Situational" commitments comprise the bulk of
policy. These enhance maintenance of the domestic political system
and make a substantial contribution to the expansion of the system's
"capabilities."[3] Tito's personal affinity for foreign relations has
committed considerable resources and energies (some surpluses)
to the external dimension of Yugoslav interests.

Hard data are available which lead us to a rather clear understanding of the complexion and general priorities of Yugoslav external
policy. Included among such variables are social, cultural, and
political dimensions which, when compiled in a single set of figures
and rankings, might be labelled "external orientation." The intimacy
of the marriage in the Yugoslav system between domestic and foreign
patterns of policy (and development) may be highlighted by a ranking
drawn from comparative data on the other apparently more cautious
socialist systems of Eastern Europe.[4] It is hoped that, viewed collectively, these indicators will estsblish the general place of foreign
relations in Yugoslav development. The next section, on foreign
business activity should complement this task by bringing into focus
the growth of the economic priority in the international dealings of
the country.

The selected set of "external orientation" variables can go a
long way toward identifying the commitment of resources to and the
priority of contemporary economic and foreign policy and its subsequent impact and momentum.[5] A brief review of the "RANK" column
on Table 10 will point summarily to the proposition at hand. Yugoslavia, through a number of strategies, methods, priorities, and circumstances, has developed a highly visible if controversial presence
in and beyond Europe. The interaction is clearly not exclusively
economic. Indeed, many political, military, cultural, and social
variables stand out very prominently, among them commitment
to diplomatic relations, immigrants and emigrants, purchases of

military equipment, tourism, and cultural exchange. The purely
statistical representation of this thrust of Yugoslav policy (indicated
by the table) does not adequately reflect the more amorphous preferences of Yugoslavs toward the world around them. From a socio-
logical and cultural perspective, there is abundant evidence of positive
popular response to and, beyond that, stimulation for increased international contact. This is, in one sense, a "soft" input (recycled if
one considers the concept of popular "response") into policy formation and conduct. Yet it is a central factor when considered in terms
of the (1) support strata of the leadership; (2) rule application and
goal attainment of the system; (3) conflict or harmony engendered
by interest articulation and aggregation; and (4) composite concept of
the pace of change and development. This affinity of Yugoslavs for
international contacts grows not only from the initiative of the leadership but also from the Yugoslav's cosmopolitan twentieth-century
history, the record of major emigration to the Western nations creating social and cultural bonds, and the pride which Yugoslavs take
in their prestigious image in the "Third World." Yugoslavs compete
enthusiastically in the sporting world, encourage profuse academic
and cultural exchanges,[6] and perform as hosts to masses of European
tourists every year.

A review of salient official foreign policy events of the past
twenty-five years indicates that foreign economic relations are crucial. Scanned chronologically and interpreted in the context of the
East-West conflict, the record reveals both a major Yugoslav dependence on external relations and a masterful balancing to avoid
political commitment growing out of this economic dependence. Table
11 reflects the shifting nature of foreign economic committments.
From the brief synopsis it is reasonably clear that the Yugoslavs
do not consider withdrawal from economic intercourse with major
world powers to be a tangible policy alternative. The specific provisions of the 1965 Reforms, based on the injection of the Yugoslav
system into the world economy and on a major commitment to diplomatic activity abroad, similarly sustain this conclusion.

The rather regular shifting of priorities and directions of
foreign economic relations results in a decidedly fluid if not unstable
and insecure policy. Since 1965, as a counterweight to this official
inconsistency, the decentralized enterprise system has constituted
a broad, massive, and "conservative" force whose ultimate interest
lies in the validity and credibility of contractual and business arrangements over time. This is a product of the substantial latitude born
by the individual economic enterprises to establish and pursue foreign
economic relations commensurate with their particular and narrowly
focused needs.

TABLE 10

Yugoslav External Orientation Variables

Variable*	Observation and Date		Rank
Items of foreign mail sent per capita	1.46	(1961)	2nd behind East Germany
Immigrants per thousand population	18	(1957-58)	2nd in East Europe behind Poland
Emigrants per thousand population	2.73	(1957-58)	2nd in East Europe behind Poland
Radios per thousand population	120.00	(1967)	11th
Passenger cars per thousand population	7.00	(1967)	6th
Tourism—total foreign visitors	3,387,430	(1968)	1st
Import of long films	285.00	(1968)	1st
Export of long films	85.00	(1968)	1st
Military personnel as percent of population	2.17	(1959)	3rd
	1.35	(1967)	–
Expenditure on defense as percent of GNP	7.30	(1959)	2nd
Number of nations from which military equipment is purchased	5.00		1st
Foreign trade (imports-exports) as percent of GNP	13.00	(1959)	1st among Communist states in 1959
Diplomatic relations (number states with)	90.00	(1970)	2nd

*Transport and Communications variables reflect substantial activity. Among those examined but not presented are: Foreign exchange receipts of enterprises of public transport, transshipment, and communications; international passenger railway transport; exports and imports of goods by railway; international sea-borne goods traffic; vessels entered seaports; passenger traffic at seaports; and number of entries of foreign motor vehicles and passengers.

Note: see also Table 4.6, Yugoslav Capability Data: Trade and Balance of Payments. Some dated figures were selected for comparative purposes.

Source: Compiled by the author.

TABLE 11

Highlights of Yugoslav Economic Relations, 1948–70

Year	Pro-Soviet	Pro-Western	Neutralist
1948		December, Belgrade announced decrease in trade with Soviets over rift	
1949		Economic agreements made with West (in particular U.S.)	
		September, American Import/Export Bank granted Yugoslavia $20 million loan	
		September, Soviet Union denounced Aid and Friendship Treaty, other East European states followed	
1950		March, Yugoslavia/West relations developed (economic and political)	
			May, Tito declared Yugoslavia "neutral" between East and West
		December, Truman authorized $38 million Marshall Plan funds for Yugoslavia	

(continued)

TABLE 11 (continued)

Year	Pro-Soviet	Pro-Western	Neutralist
1951		November, agreement with U.S. to supply arms	
1952		July, U.S. decided to send Yugoslavia heavy military equipment, including jet aircraft	
		October, Djilas criticized Stalin's economic theses	
1955	January, USSR and Yugoslavia signed formal trade agreement		
	July, Soviet trade increased 60 percent by agreement		
1957	July, talks in Moscow restored $250 million in Soviet aid to Yugoslavia	February, Khrushchev confirmed new Yugoslavia rift. No more "economic favors" from USSR	
1958		December, U.S. agreed to let Yugoslavia purchase $95 million of surplus agricultural goods	
1961		October, U.S. revealed sale of jet fighters to Yugoslavia	

Year			
1963	April, U.S. moved to drastically cut U.S. aid to Yugoslavia September, Yugoslavia/USSR conclude vast trade agreement		November, Gheorghiu-Dej visited Belgrade. Yugoslavia-Romanian relations cemented with "Iron Gate" agreement
1964	September, Tito stated that Yugoslavia would participate in Comecon	April, U.S. announced huge wheat deal with Yugoslavia July, Yugoslavia/West Germany economic agreements. Foreign employment for Yugoslavs in spite of lack of diplomatic relations	
1965		July, new economic reforms officially announced. Many foreign economic relations implications	April, Yugoslav sources announced Yugoslav foreign debt of billion dollars
1969		February, Yugoslavia and West Germany concluded economic treaty	

The international presence of the Yugoslavs has been, at least in large measure, the product and responsibility of the economic, or more precisely, the management elite. Enterprise direktors, economic chamber personnel, and other national economic experts have had a major influence on policy via two essential developments: (1) the decentralization of the economy has empowered them to initiate foreign relationships in their own interest; and (2) the basic designs and perceptions of needs of the national governmental elite and the economic elite were shared and through the development of policy came to appear very harmonious. This suggests that confluence and mutual reinforcement existed in the period from 1966 to 1971 on matters relating to the type, rate, and costs of change in the economic system.

This overview suggests that Yugoslavs and the various levels of their system have dedicated a substantial portion of the resources of the people and the state to external relations. This point can be made more emphatically if the record is examined in comparison with other East European Communist states. It is in this milieu that the economic elite operating within the bounds of the Yugoslav domestic system (discussed in earlier chapters of this research) has effected a most dramatic change in the conventional pattern and conduct of Communist states. This experiment in the growth of foreign business activity and the relatively free atmosphere to set needs, goals, priorities, and alternatives at the microlevel has opened a new focus for comparative analysis. The next section probes the crucial aspects of this new development and concludes with some propositions about the implications of these changes.

DIMENSIONS OF FOREIGN BUSINESS ACTIVITY

Foreign business activity is superficially reflected by trading patterns. Yugoslavia's economic character and visibility in the international community share many features with a large cross-section of rapidly industrializing and developing nations. However, few such nations realize the pace of economic growth and even fewer match that growth with a political efficacy which buttresses the ability of the system to accommodate the dislocation incumbent in such sharp and complete systemic change. Punctuating this uniqueness, the Yugoslav system has, in the philosophical context of Marxism, premeditated official and operational policy designed to loosen central governmental control over foreign business relations. This dismantling of planning mechanisms is exceptional among industrialized states (a cogent argument can be made that the reverse is the norm) and even more rare among those developing states beset by inflation, severe balance of payments problems, and other basic and overt signs of economic dislocation.

Muhamed Hadzic, Yugoslav Federal Secretary for Foreign Trade, reported in 1971 that, "Yugoslavia's commodity exchange with foreign countries may be described as extremely significant. . . . Its volume and tendencies also graphically reflect the basic determinants of the position of Yugoslavia's economy in international trade."[7] Foreign trade in 1970 registered a remarkable 27 percent (17 percent when corrected for price inflation) increase over 1969 which is the highest annual rate of growth in the history of the Socialist Federal Republic of Yugoslavia. The raw figures of foreign trade exchange was roughly 4.6 billion dollars, or 25 percent of the "total social product" of the economy. Hadzic's evaluation continues, "this gives indication of the considerable dependence of our economy, and especially foreign trade, on world trends which were restless last year and marked by inflationary manifestations."[8]

As one might anticipate in a rapidly developing country, the balance or imbalance of payments is a continuing and earnest concern (see Table 12). Yugoslavia is fortunate that much of this inequity is compensated for by "noncommodity proceeds." This includes "invisible earnings" drawn from areas in which Yugoslavia is especially active. Examples include tourism, the shipping industry, construction work abroad, and remittances of wages earned by Yugoslav workers employed abroad. Of the twenty million Yugoslavs, nearly one million work abroad. The Financial Times recently assessed, "remittances from the million or so Yugoslavs now working abroad—which will automatically increase following devaluation—do of course reduce the deficit to manageable proportions."[9] Available data indicate that during the first nine months of 1969 Yugoslavs working abroad sent home $140 million. Other benefits include training, hard currency payment, and Western pay scales.[10] Official sources maintain that they are fully satisfied with export volume but admit that the sprinting technology and growth of consumerism have thrust imports to a level warranting some serious reflection by the system-at-large.[11] High level Yugoslav alarm is modified by the realization that this situation is largely a function of other factors, some of which are beyond their control or which involve costs they perceive to be offset by potential gains. Specifically, the rapidly developing accumulation of problems inherent in the structure of the economy, problems of foreign currency and the foreign trade system, and those stemming from noneconomic trends at home and abroad, are among the most often cited. Confidence is based on the fact that Yugoslavia has undeveloped sources of many raw materials which it now imports. Patterns of manufacturing are also beginning to emerge which could offset the importation of vast quantities of consumer goods through domestic production.

TABLE 12

1970—Foreign Trade Record
(in percents)

		Import	Export
(a)	Percent of Growth Rate		
	Trade deficit = $1.16 billion	34.7	13.9
(b)	Percent of Total Imports		
	Manufacturing	64.4	—
	Equipment	21.1	—
	Consumer goods	13.9	—
	Other	0.6	—
(c)	Growth Index 1969/1970		
	Industrially advanced countries in the West	115.5	114.9
	Socialist countries of Comecon	119.4	116.6
	Developing countries	93.2	118.3
	Share in 1970		
	Industrially advanced countries in the West	56.3	68.9
	Socialist countries of Comecon	32.4	20.7
	Developing countries	11.3	10.4
(d)	Targets of the Federal Assembly Resolution on Economic Policy, 1971		
	Growth Rate	7.0	13.5

Source: Review of International Affairs, Documentation Section, no. 504, April 5, 1971, p. 13-14.

A brief but clear explanation of the inflationary spiral of the Yugoslav situation is offered.

Last year in Yugoslavia, spending increased palpably in all sectors—personal, investment, and budgetary. This led to a greater issue of money and, most importantly, caused a higher rise in prices than was the case in the majority of other countries. In consequence, importing and marketing on the internal market became more attractive than exporting.[12]

The hard facts of inflation in 1970 are sketched by the following figures:[13]

Nominal wages increased	19%
Real wages increased	7%
Cost of living increased	11%
Productivity increased	6%
Agricultural output decreased	7%
Industrial output increased	9%

The emphasis on trade relations with Western Europe is illustrated by the fact that Italy and West Germany are by far the dominant trading partners for the Yugoslavs. The Soviet Union is third followed by Great Britain and France.[14] The bulk of the balance of payments deficit may be located by examining the Western European accounts. Other financial cooperation is impressive. The Brandt government in Bonn and the Pompidou government in Paris have made substantial financial overtures, but the most important to date is an Italian loan of $75 million to enable Yugoslavia to respond to some short-term commitments and difficulties. The fervor with which the Yugoslavs are opening European contacts may be reflected by the fact that in 1970 Tito personally visited every EEC country and has, since the Czech invasion and the Lusaka Conference, forged a new European emphasis in the foreign policy of Yugoslavia.[15]

One financial analyst recently wrote, "Small wonder the EEC has been proclaimed 'our most important partner' in trade as in other forms of economic co-operation."[16] Michael Simmons, Financial Times correspondent, supplied his rationale by pointing to (1) the inclination of the Yugoslavs to favor the West over the East; (2) the three-year nonpreferential trade agreement with the EEC providing easier markets for Yugoslav exports; and (3) the change in status of the above agreement to a "preferential" level (July 1971) "to the ideological as well as commercial delight of the Yugoslavs." The trend, clearly established over the past three years, is toward "more direct" commercial and technological cooperation.

This economic collaboration does not begin to tell the full story or, more accurately, the emerging story of business activity between Yugoslavia and the Western industrialized states. Accurate and complete data are unavailable because of the informal and autonomous nature of corporate arrangements and meetings. However, we can gather a sense of the magnitude and direction of such efforts by surveying the trade literature and by interviewing key personnel.

Apart from loans, credits, and aid which have at various times been a critical input into the economic and political recovery and growth of Socialist Yugoslavia, the first bidirectional economic

arrangement, were of the licensing type. Hardly a "mature" or co-
equal arrangement, this generally provided for the assembly, inside
Yugoslavia, of foreign products made from imported parts. It was a
step ahead, but not one which was received with any great enthusiasm
by the more aggressive Yugoslav managers. Such deals bring on the
label "screwdriver" industries, which in the system describe a situation in which the only Yugoslav contribution and function is the assemblage, the actual labor to produce the finished product. The auto
industry in Yugoslavia was a prime example. But it is also an example of the maturing relationship between foreign and domestic busi-
nesses. Crvena Zastava began in this way but, through the cooperation
of the Fiat (Italian) corporation, has now established itself as the
only major producer of completely Yugoslav cars. Today, the two
most popular models are manufactured from parts which are nearly
all Yugoslav-made while three other models are partially constructed
with domestically produced parts. The success of the Zastava must
be laid at the doorstep of the Italians. They have enthusiastically
backed the fledgling industry in Yugoslavia through massive outlays
of financing and a very flexible business policy vis-à-vis their Yugoslav partners. Last year the total Fiat investment rose to $17 million,
the largest of the joint ventures to be undertaken in Yugoslavia to
date. Their share of the Yugoslav car market is approximately 90
percent which, if nothing else, attests to the sound business wisdom
in the Fiat deal. Similar arrangements on a less developed level
have now crystallized between Pretis and NSU (West German auto
maker), Tomos and Citroen (French auto maker controlled by Fiat),
and IMV and BMC (British Motor Company). Of these only Pretis
has reached the goal of manufacturing parts to be used in assemblage
and their current level is about 20 percent. Apart from these established joint efforts, Renault joined the market in 1972; Opel (W. Germany), Saab and Volvo (both Swedish), and Mazda (Japanese) are very
near agreements with various Yugoslav firms. Generally, the government has remained in the background though it has made and enforced
regulations (tariffs) which, on the one hand, seriously discourage the
purchase of foreign-made and assembled vehicles, and on the other,
sanctions and encouraged business ventures of the type described.
One exception to this principle is to be found in the purchase of Eastern European cars. Yugoslavia has a favorable trade balance with
these states, but the lower prestige of Eastern products has held
down consumption of East European cars and other products.

 The auto industry stands as one of the prominent examples of
innovative business activity, but it is only one of many. American
interest has been stimulated significantly by a meeting held on
Tito's winter trip to the United States in 1971. Out of that meeting
at Blair House in which Tito, Secretary of Commerce Maurice Stans,

and numerous leaders of American industry participated, a new commitment to allow more than 49 percent ownership by foreign firms participating in joint ventures was made by Tito.[17] The response was convincing. Allis-Chalmers, Greyhound Corporation, the Borden Corporation, Pan American, and Gulf and Western have moved to the "advanced stages" of negotiation with Yugoslav firms.[18] Other major business interests are reported to be negotiating less visibly. American commercial interest in Yugoslavia is not restricted to joint investment, though it would appear on the surface to be the most enduring form of business commitment. One such variation which received much attention in Western business circles in 1970 was the sales arrangement between McDonnell Douglas Corporation and JAT, the Yugoslav airline. Douglas Aircraft sold eleven DC-9 jets to the Yugoslavs for $35 million. Douglas received payment arranged through loans and credits with U.S. commercial banks, the Export-Import Bank, and through their own financing company. The less common feature of this deal and the one that illustrates the eagerness of American firms to do business with Yugoslav enterprises is the commitment Douglas made to help market $9 million worth of Yugoslav goods in the United States. By marketing about 25 percent of the total cost of the aircraft, Yugoslav concerns about a more serious balance of payments problem were dispelled. In fact, Douglas Aircraft purchased $40,000 of Yugoslav ham for use in its own cafeterias to give the program an initial boost.

British Aircraft Corporation was also in competition for this sale. The British offered a complete barter deal to the Yugoslavs, an arrangement common in dealings between firms of these two countries. Interestingly, numerous interviews with a multi-national cross-section of corporate elites who have dealt with, and are planning to deal with the Yugoslavs, suggest that Americans are, in the main, significantly more positive and more confident about (1) the ability of the Yugoslavs to succeed and (2) the direction and wisdom of their socio-economic experiment. The British were the most reserved, while the West Germans' sentiment was closer to that of the Americans. Britain's relative caution, bordering on reluctance, has not quelled all interest. As noted in an earlier chapter, Dunlop has undertaken a major joint venture with a Yugoslav counterpart. M. M. Markovic, Yugoslav Economic Minister in London during the late 1960s, can attest to the regular interest of Britain firms in both trade and joint ventures. Initial inquiries are often channelled through his office.

The record of formalized joint investment agreements may provide us with a meaningful indicator of foreign business interest in Yugoslavia in addition to Yugoslav priorities and preferences among potential business contacts abroad. Ventures registered in

1968 and 1969 totalled 15 and were distributed in the following manner: Italy 7, France 2, and one each for Sweden, United States, Bel-
gium, West Germany, East Germany, and Czechoslovakia. Thirteen
of the first fifteen ventures were made with Western European partners (including the one U.S. venture).[19] The second fifteen reflected
the same general pattern except that West Germany increased her
investment to become the single most intense investor. As suggested
by Miodrag Sukijasovic, a leading Yugoslav scholar on joint investment, in an interview with this researcher, the principal aim of this
kind of business arrangement is to secure technology, including management expertise, and capital, in that order. This proposition is certainly sustained by the above list of chosen partners. It may also be
significant that the statutes and regulations which are relevant to
the program of foreign investment in Yugoslavia are among the most
actively revised and reviewed of all legal provisions in the socialist
state. Tito's statement in 1971 signalled even greater revisions and
flexibility which have now found their way into the law. It should be
reemphasized that while inquiries from abroad are often channelled
through economic offices of the government or through organizations
like the International Investment Corporation for Yugoslavia or the
Yugoslav American Corporation, which are especially designed to
perform this function, the initiative from the domestic side is from
the local enterprise. Banks play a very central role in the contracts
and other arrangements which grow out of initial contacts. Yugoslav banks, vested with considerably more autonomy than was the
case before the Reforms, now participate as equals with their Western counterparts in formalizing provisions of their joint venture.[20]
        The inclination to look westward for partners is primarily but
not exclusively economic. A high-ranking Yugoslav politician very
familiar with the Russians is reported by the Economist to have said:

> In contrast to those tame western imperialists who re-
> quire so little from Yugoslavia and do not interfere at all,
> the ones who sit in the Kremlin demand too much and in-
> terfere incessantly. The Russians and their friends, par-
> ticularly the East Germans, are forever on the phone
> about the sort of things our press writes about them.
> They can't get into their heads that, unlike them, we
> no longer control our journalists from above and simply
> cannot tell them what to write about anything, including
> the Soviet Union and other block countries. Of course,
> as politicians, we are sometimes sorry that we no longer
> have this control. But when occasionally we try to guide
> journalists, it always costs us too much. After years of
> being muzzled, our journalists and broadcasters are so

jealous of their newly won independence, and often so
bloody-minded in its defence, that they will go out of their
way to say things that we are sure to disapprove of—just
to show they are no longer government stooges. But those
chaps in Moscow and east Berlin will never understand
that.

The Economist article continues, "The Jugoslavs are sensitive about
this kind of interference from Moscow and other Warsaw pact capitals, because they know that it does not come from academic critics
with no ulterior motives. It comes from hard-headed, tough men
who have already invaded Czechoslovakia, and cited Czechoslovakia's
free press as one of the reasons for their invasion."[21] This aversion
is offset by economic rationale which spotlights the advantages of
economic relations with East European nations.

Joint investment contracts with East European partners are
the exception. We noted that two of the first fifteen were with socialist countries. Both the East German and Czech deals were of major
financial proportions and were made in industries in which the partner's technological expertise is well recognized. It is not surprising
that such agreements are few in number. Firms in East Europe do
not have control over their investment funds nor do they have the
facility to accumulate such funds. In practice then, Eastern firms
can bring neither capital nor major technological know-how to the
bargain.[22] Beyond these general but not universal rules, it is well
established that one of the bases for the Soviet-Yugoslav split in
1948 was the distaste which Yugoslavs had for the "joint stock companies." The post-war Yugoslav caution seems in retrospect worthy
of no small amount of praise especially if the Czechoslovak economic
experience (1948-68) is a reasonable parallel.

In contrast, Yugoslav trade is consummated on the basis of
mutual business interests. The Yugoslav option, East or West, is
enviable from a trade perspective and comparisons become inevitable.
The trading thrusts between Yugoslavia and the two areas strike two
distinct postures. Yugoslav-Comecon trade (by volume) has grown
more cautiously than Yugoslavia-EEC trade. In fact, with the former, the percentage of total trade has periodically declined. Making
this same comparison, the Financial Times reported; "Trade with
the COMECON area presents a completely different picture. Yugoslav
exports in that direction have been steadily falling in recent years
to reach 31 percent of the total last year, while imports from it have
fallen from more than 40 percent five years ago to just over 21 percent last year [1970]."[23] The alarm evident over this rapid decline
is reflected in a new set of five-year agreements which could have
the projected benefit of significantly increasing trade by 1975. The

111

success of these plans remains contingent upon the clear perception by the Yugoslav enterprise elite that such an increase is in their interest. A brief review of the apparent advantages and disadvantages of Comecon trade and economic cooperation follows.

The relative quality of goods and the production of consumer-oriented goods gives Yugoslavia a very competitive place in the East European market. The low quality and availability of such products in East Europe also means that it is possible for Yugoslav firms to sell lower quality items which are unmarketable either in West Europe or at home. Second, Yugoslavia's "soft" currency problem is abrogated by the willingness of East European states to accept either barter or the soft currency itself. Third, by straddling the demarcation line between East and West geographically, economically, and politically, Yugoslavia can reap the benefits of retrading items from the West through Yugoslavia to the East and vice versa. In some cases Yugoslav firms have a hand in the manufacture of the product (example, Zastava building cars), in other cases it is strictly a re-packing and relabelling operation. In any case, it is profitable, though as the bloc countries begin to open new economic relations with the West this feature of the trading pattern may be reshaped. Fourth, the favorable balance of trade with Communist states is an added inducement to continue the imbalance in Yugoslavia's favor. Fifth, solid transportation systems connect Yugoslavia and other Eastern countries. These include the Danube River system, a well equipped airline, and respectable highway links with most of these countries. Her port facilities also contribute to the economic attractiveness of trans-shipping commodities via Yugoslavia.[24] Collectively, these create an additional incentive for trade through the manifest discrimination which grows from the state trading relationship. A recent study of this phenomenon for the years 1966-68 draws some relevant conclusions.

> Yugoslavia discriminated against the Bloc countries in both the export and import package. . . . In all import instances, Yugoslavia received the bundle of goods for a lower price than a like bundle would have cost on Western markets. Likewise, on all but eight of the twenty-four export bundles . . . Yugoslavia was able to charge the Bloc nations a higher price than a similar bundle would have commanded on Western markets. . . . Yugoslavia, in her trade with the Bloc nations, gained a monopoly profit amounting to 28.8 per cent (over the three year period) of the trade turnover revalued at Western prices.[25]

This study goes on to hypothesize that the ability to discriminate in this manner is inversely related to the degree of dependence of the Yugoslavs on trade with those countries. Given that Yugoslavia has clear options, it follows that Yugoslavia can and does effectively discriminate in pricing with the East Europeans. West European discrimination against East Europe and Yugoslav "most favored nation" status coupled with her GATT (General Agreement on Tariffs and Trade) participation reinforces her capability.[26]

The state monopoly trading system upon which this advantage depends has drawbacks in the context of recent Yugoslav reforms. In trading relationships with East European countries the Yugoslav government acts as the agent of the firm actually buying or selling the commodity because it is only in this way that reasonable financial guarantees can be secured. Early in the development of the Yugoslav decentralized system, enterprise direktors legally confronted state trading agencies from other Communist states. In most cases, the individual firms met with failure, leading to the common practice of requesting the Yugoslav state, through its government agencies, to act in the local enterprise's behalf. This system has proved adequate, but the enterprise direktors look upon it as a nuisance and a cumbersome bureaucratic detour. Timing and effective communications, two elements of the business pattern receiving greater attention in the management of contemporary Yugoslav firms, are the first casualties in this state to state trading relationship. For this structural reason, enterprises prefer trading relationships with the West. An expert source puts this argument in these terms:

> The Belgrade view remains, so far as trade is concerned, one of qualified superiority to COMECON. The mechanics by which the East European countries are forced to construct their bi-lateral trading agreements with Yugoslavia are seen as obsolete, and the complaints one hears from the "market socialist" exporters, frustrated in their endeavors to meet the elusive end-user, echo strangely the complaints that one also hears in, say, London, of a broadly similar nature.[27]

Other disadvantages appear frequently in the Yugoslav press and in official sources. Yugoslav cooperation with Comecon is based on an agreement signed in 1964 and worked out some time before that. It is dated and does not reflect the needs and relationships which were created by the major reforms in the economic system of Yugoslavia. Worst of all, it provides no entree to the decision-making authority at the microlevel—the enterprise. Still other problems develop because Yugoslavia imports mostly raw materials

while she exports finished goods to East Europe. Fifty-nine percent
of her imports from this area are raw materials; 22 percent of her
exports are general consumer goods and 21 percent more are ac-
counted for by equipment and shipping. In the short run, this is an
advantageous position to be in, but critics argue that it inhibits Yugoslav capital investment in opening indigenous sources of raw materials.
A member of the Federal Executive Council recently listed the factors
adversely affecting Yugoslav/Comecon trade: "excessively high prices
of certain commodities, their unsatisfactory quality and assortment,
shortage of spare parts and lack of necessary technical documentation,
unsatisfactory terms of delivery and difficulties in the purchase of
non-serial equipment. Other difficulties stem from the system of
clearing accounts which has many shortcomings."[28] Finally, the
bilateral system of trade now functioning presupposes long-term
state agreements, fixed contingents and prices, and strictly balanced
deliveries which in total are unrealistically simple given the maturing
and complex, that is to say, decentralized, system in Yugoslavia.

In spite of these difficulties trading contracts are in evidence
among many of the largest and strongest enterprises in Yugoslavia.
A partial list is found on Table 13. The task of solving or repond-
ing to these problems of trading and contracts are, under the new
system, to be handled by the economic enterprises themselves, the
economic chambers, industrial associations, and the banks. It is a
stiff test for these new centers of authority.

Trade with "developing" nations is more limited than trade
with either the East or the West. Increased trade and technical exchange with these nations is a political as well as an economic objective. The Yugoslavs deal on positive terms with such states and
make a point of buying from them both finished and raw goods. The
problems are as diverse as the nations grouped by the "developing"
label, yet Yugoslav enterprises and exporting companies have made
considerable gains in recent years. The Federal Assembly Resolution on Economic Policy for 1971 prescribed that, "It is important
for us to intensify trade with developing countries even further . . .
by the achievement of an agreement on preferences in favor of these
countries."[29] The principal aim of this government policy is to
"create conditions facilitating a tangible decrease in the deficit of
the current balance of payments."

To add yet another indication of increased Yugoslav involvement in foreign business activity, the two most recent Import-Export
Directories published by the Publicity Office of the SPK are compared. Among other kinds of information the directory lists the
enterprises which have been active in either import or export ventures. Essential data on the firm and the commodities exchanged
are included. A survey of the 1969 Directory yielded a count of 716

TABLE 13

Major Yugoslav-Comecon Business Contracts
(April 1971)

Country	Yugoslav Enterprise	Home Office
Bulgaria	Teleoptik	Zemun
	Rade Koncar	Zagreb
Czechoslovakia	Duro Dakovic	Slavonski Brod
	Rade Koncar	Zagreb
	Zorka	Subotica
	Tito	Skopje
	Nis Electronic Works	Nis
	Energoinvest	Sarajevo
East Germany	Iskra	Kranj
	Prvomajska	Zagreb
	Masinoimpeks	Zagreb
Hungary	Pobeda	Novi Sad
	Zmaj	Zemun
	Ikarus	Zemun
	Sever	Subotica
	Obod	Centinje
	IMT	Belgrade
	Nis Electronic Works	Nis
Poland	Crvena zastava	Kragujevac
	Magnohrom	Kraljevo
Romania	Torpedo	Rijeka
	Pobeda	Novi Sad
	Masino-union	Belgrade
Soviet Union	Crvena zastava	Kragujevac
	Travnik	Travnik

Source: Compiled by the author.

115

Yugoslav enterprises that were active internationally. The next directory, issued as the 1970-71 edition, listed 851 such enterprises, an increase slightly greater than 15 percent. A tally of International Fairs and Exhibitions indicates 21 events in 1969, 29 events in 1970. Banking offices and representatives is another category. In 1969 there were 14 foreign branches while in 1970 the number grew to 23. Finally, in checking for SPK Offices abroad, the earlier figure was 13, the later 29. All of this leads to the conclusion that a dramatic commitment, at an extraordinary pace, has been made to foreign business activity.

IMPLICATIONS

The commitment noted above derives from the decentralization of the system which has emancipated individual firms to pursue foreign contacts along the lines that their particular needs dictate. An interesting reflection may be found in the Financial Times special edition on Yugoslavia: "As still more devolution in the running of the nation's economy is being planned, they must also be wondering just how they can now develop a precise trading policy."[30] The uncertainty is now a fact of life for those who would seek a cogent foreign economic policy. The system has gambled on the premise that what is good for the economic enterprises at the local level will produce good for the development and growth of the system at large. It is an unorthodox approach for a Communist state, but one whose track record so far is quite healthy.

For a system that has undertaken to experiment with the international economic system, we can be reasonably certain that the trade statistics and the joint venture contracts are but the visible part of the iceberg. If a practical measure could be found for ongoing business "activity," the importance of this level of economic decision-making could be even more impressively established. As one searches for the more obscure signs of interaction, it is well to remember the types of changes in both organization and personnel which have taken place at the microlevel, to remember the linkages established for direktors and economic elites to influence national policy, and to recall the fundamental changes broached in Chapter 4. With these as a foundation, the process of reviewing and analyzing the propositions of this chapter is drawn into focus.

Yugoslav foreign business activity in the area of nonindustrial interaction is characterized by (1) manpower working abroad and the repatriation of subsequent income; (2) tourism; (3) shipping and transport (retrading); and (4) general participation in the OECD, EEC, EFTA, Comecon, Unctad, and GATT. These dimensions contribute to the over-all picture, but are peripheral to and/or reinforcements of the principal thrust of foreign business activity. Industrial or corporate dialogue is the core of Yugoslav international economic relationships. Investment agencies and offices, joint venture contracts, technological consultation, and management development programs and consultations are all signs of this emerging priority.

Tensions and conflicts persist, reflecting both the magnitude and direction of developing Yugoslav patterns of international business activity. Pricing and marketing discrimination in East Europe stands juxtaposed to the "proper" relations between socialist states. The fundamentally contrasted alternatives between increased exchange with the Eastern and Western states and economic organizations create apprehension about the forms of domestic political and economic structures. A hypothesis is offered that the resolution of this choice, considered in the long run, will shape the nature and functional relationships within the system. Decentralization is a more amenable organizational scheme to business relations with the West, while a return to centralization would predispose international involvement with the East. A final and in some ways independent problem is the dilemma of pursuing increased interaction with the "emerging" or "developing" Third World nations at the cost of tight relations with the two "power blocs." During the 1960s the drift of Yugoslav policy was in the direction of the Afro-Asian nations. In spite of early successes, the political zeal for a Third World emphasis in policy waned. The collective voice of direktors in Yugoslavia also became more resonant, rekindling an interest in an expanded European relationship. The 1970s seem clearly marked by this shift. One may speculate that since the Reforms and the growth of joint investment, Yugoslav confidence with regard to their collective ability to compete in and contribute to the international community of "developed" states (referred to previously as a "club-like" organization) alleviates the commanding need to opt into commerce and to develop the economic system along the lines of Afro-Asian models.

It may be of considerable consequence that ideological guidance for these policy decisions is a "non-issue". The absence of this conflict is a critical feature of the pattern of foreign economic policy. Increasingly the rationale for policy is articulated in terms of Yugoslav interests, general economic development, and the commitment to the policy of decision-making authority at the microlevel or "decentralization through workers' self-management." Philosophical systems are criticized for their inflexibility. Roger Garaudy's writing and experience vis-à-vis the Soviet Union was a particularly prominent subject in Yugoslavia. Doctrine, as the vehicle for passing controls down through the hierarchy of the system, is officially discouraged. Only doctrine broached in the broadest social terms is to be used as a guide for policy. Apparently foreign economic relations are no exception.

Three basic implications follow from the discussion in this chapter. First, Yugoslavia has developed a dependence on, and commitment to, active, aggressive, foreign economic contact. As noted earlier, however, this dependence is diffuse—parcelled out among the various areas and states within those areas. It consciously integrated its economy (price structure) into the world market and into the less than precise international division of labor. Having made that decision, Yugoslavia's economy became more stable as a whole but vulnerable to the machinations of the established world economic powers. This said, Yugoslavia has balanced its commitments very carefully. Its ability to continue to restrain over-commitment to one bloc or another is diminishing rapidly with decentralization. For this reason, it follows that the balance will tip in favor of Western contacts and that decentralization will thereby pick up a momentum which will be hard to break.

Second, phenomena which give form to international business activity, including dialogues, contracts, and financing, indicate that the men involved in such activity have accepted a number of values which are shared with their opposite members in Western economic systems. Direktors whose base of authority and scope of direct responsibility is limited to the microeconomic unit, the enterprise, reflect an essential pragmatism which contributes to their ability to achieve their and their enterprise's immediate goals. The practitioner, the businessman, is confronted by negotiations, production management, marketing, financing, and so forth on a tangible and daily basis. On a scale from technician to philosopher the typical direktor would most certainly fall close to the "technician." He is judged by concrete performance and, to the extent that this is the case, is inherently a pragmatist. In foreign business relations the modes of conduct and the types of relationships are structured in a classic pattern. The Yugoslavs conform and open these new dimensions or they resist and are frustrated in their search for technology, capital, commodities, and markets. The record in general illustrates an adept Yugoslav adjustment to this challenge.

Finally, from the implications above, a proposition could be offered with regard to the encompassing effect of foreign business activity on domestic social processes in Yugoslavia. This intercourse with both men and systems nurtures a system modification effect. Its impact on the Yugoslav system is to blunt radical change, avert a sharp reversal of ongoing policies, and create and reinforce an identification with the structure and functioning of the system as it takes shape. Foreign commitments and contacts prolong the time required to make changes, introduce new stabilizing elements or

considerations into the decision-making process, and open the domestic system to more gradual change on the example of foreign systems.
In the main, then, the decision to look outward has matured the system-at-large and has exposed the components in the system (enterprise, chambers, and so forth) to the organizational and functional alternatives already tested by other economic systems.

With these hypothesized implications drawn from the clear trend toward greater international business activity, this research concludes its examination of specific dimensions of the Yugoslav system and moves now to the task of drawing some cogent and meaningful conclusions.

NOTES

1. Richard Farkas, "Contemporary Yugoslav Foreign Policy," in Kuhlman (ed.), The Foreign Policies of Eastern Europe: Domestic and International Determinants, forthcoming.

2. Ibid.

3. "Capabilities" is interpreted very broadly to include flexibility, momentum, prestige, and symbolic policy-making as well as the more tangible "raw" capabilities reflected in Table 5.

4. Other East European state systems have exercised more apparent caution in linking (either conceptually or publicly) their patterns of foreign and domestic policy. Rationale for this inhibition is offered in many scholarly efforts, but Gitelman succintly presents the case for explicit dichotimization in The Diffusion of Political Innovation: From Eastern Europe to the Soviet Union, Sage Professional Paper, Beverly Hills, 1971.

5. Table 10 is a discriminating list of variables drawn from Yugoslav statistical reports. One will note that more recent data are available but particular years were selected to enable a comparison to be made with other socialist states. "External orientation" is an encompassing and imprecise concept which is given some substance by the variables selected. Communication, mobility, contact, and dependence all may be subsumed by the general subject heading.

6. Comparatively, Yugoslavia is the most active East European nation in the area of academic and cultural exchange. If loosely defined, this includes a quantitative comparison with the USSR which when proportions are considered aptly punctuates Yugoslavia's commitment to such interaction.

7. Muhamed Hadzic, "Present Trends and Problems in Yugoslav Foreign Trade," Review of International Affairs, #504, April 5, 1971, p. 13.

8. Ibid.

9. Michael Simmons, "Radical Devolution of Economic Control," The Financial Times, April 26, 1971, p. 12.

10. Eric Bourne, "Yugoslavs Migrate to Western Europe for Steady Jobs," Christian Science Monitor, January 7, 1970, p. 4.

11. Annual O.E.C.D. and Economist appraisals of the Yugoslav economic experience highlight this particular development and more fully illuminate its implications.

12. Hadzic, op. cit., p. 13.

13. Simmons, loc. cit., p. 12.

14. Hadzic, op. cit., p. 14. The most recent data (1970) indicate that Italy is Yugoslavia's largest customer, the USSR is second, but in sales to Yugoslavia, West Germany is first followed by Italy and the USSR in that order. At the end of 1970, a Yugoslav-Soviet agreement was signed which projects an increase in turnover by 35 percent by 1975.

15. Reported by the Times (London), October 6, 1970, p. 8.

16. Michael Simmons, "The Debate Rages Over Devaluation Effects," The Financial Times, April 26, 1971, p. 14.

17. Ibid. p. 14.

18. David Andelman, "U.S. Units Study Yugoslavia Deal," New York Times, January 1, 1972, p. 25.

19. Four sources are particularly useful in providing detailed information about Yugoslav joint ventures.

Committee for Invisible Transactions, Foreign Investment in Yugoslavia, Organization for Economic Co-operation and Development, Paris, 1970.

Wolfgang Friedmann and Leo Mates (eds.), Joint Business Ventures of Yugoslav Enterprises and Foreign Firms, Kultura, Beograd, 1968.

Institute of Comparative Law, Laws on Joint Investments of Enterprises, Buducnost, Beograd, 1967.

Miodrag Sukujasovic, Yugoslav Foreign Investment Legislation at Work: Experiences So Far, Oceana, Belgrade, 1970.

20. J. J. Hauvonen, "Money and Banking in Yugoslavia," Finance and Development Quarterly, International Monetary Fund, Washington, D.C., Vol. 8, No. 4, December 1971, pp. 24-30.

21. "Yugoslavia," The Economist, August 21, 1971, p. viii.

22. Naturally, this generalization is vulnerable in a few marked areas of East European technological leadership. East German and Czech excellence in machine tools, petrochemicals, and metallurgy might serve as exceptions in one regard. Certainly, the Soviet Union is able to offer (though with greater political intricacies than a capitalist system) capital and know-how. The point of essential significance here is that Yugoslavia is generally at the technological level of sophistication that it can handle much of the most advanced

technology which other system may offer it. In this sense it has the base to accept and, if you will, shop for technology. The comparative statement in the text is offered in this light. The conclusion which may follow from the recent Yugoslav experience is that the West can offer more credible technological know-how and less encumbered capital on acceptable terms economically and politically defined by the Yugoslavs themselves.

23. Simmons, "Debate Rages Over Devaluation Effects," p. 14. Based on 1970 data. Some discrepancies exist in the figures though they are not major. An article in the Review of International Affairs reported the figures 30 percent (exports) and 24 percent (imports) for the same year.

24. A review of trade advantages for East Europe may be found in "Economic Cooperation with the COMECON Countries," Review of International Affairs, #505, April 20, 1971, pp. 25-27.

25. "The Effects of State Trading," a chapter from a dissertation on Discrimination and State Monopoly Trading, University of Virginia, 1971, pp. 113-114.

26. General Agreement on Tariffs and Trade. The Yugoslavs consider this convention one of the pillars of their economic foreign policy and indeed of their foreign policy generally. They continue to be very active in subsequent rounds of GATT negotiations.

27. Simmons, Financial Times, p. 14.

28. Dragisa Dokovic, "Economic Cooperation with the COMECON Countries," Review of International Affairs, #505, April 20, 1971, p. 26.

29. Hadzic, "Present Trends and Problems in Yugoslavia's Foreign Trade," p. 14.

30. Simmons, "Debate Rages Over Devaluation Effects," Financial Times, p. 14.

6

REVIEW AND
SYNTHESIS

This research was designed to examine the political implications and ramifications of basic changes and potential changes in the economic system of contemporary Yugoslavia. Emphasis was placed on the perspective provided by the examination of systemic change evident on all levels of economic activity within the society as well as considering the significance of external factors. The single greatest challenge is to fuse the problems and prospects of the various levels into a meaningful analytic whole. The "levels" are actually distinct strata of the society in which decisions on the nature and magnitude of economic planning and execution are made. Specifically, those which this study has found productive are: the enterprise, republic, nation, and the international community.

The previous chapters have examined these levels at which the economic and political elements in the system must ameliorate themselves to achieve systemic and localized goals. Withstanding a number of distinctive features at the respective levels, central patterns emerge, reflecting a consistent direction in the metamorphosis of Yugoslavia and the East European socialist states. With these empirically investigated phenomena as guidelines, a prognosis is offered. Each principal component of this research effort is reviewed with cognizance that change in the East European subsystem is imminent in the 1970s and 1980s and its course is central to the dispositions of the major powers of Europe.

Proposition 1. An economic (at some levels "business") ethos is fast becoming a determinant of economic, social, and political relationships in the system. This ethos is reflected in and is a function of (a) the goals of the system, (b) the types of acceptable solutions to economic and political problems, and (c) the attitude of politicians, economic managers, and the general public toward "politics" and the "system." Manifestations of this development are (1) popularization nurturing identification and stability; (2) a decrease in the number of purely political criteria for solutions to basic problems; (3) a realism about objectives and the probability of achieving them; and (4) a pragmatism that pervades the system. To this analyst most of these conditions, if accurately perceived, are essentially healthy and bode well for the longevity and flexibility of the system.

Proposition 2. The administrative and functional division of "economics" and "politics" creates a real tension in the system. Yugoslav ideological positions have rejected such a separation. It is nonetheless real, and it forces the establishment to provide formal and informal patterns or channels of accommodation and responsiveness. The men of both groups in the system must ameliorate themselves to the tasks and objectives of the others. The Yugoslav case is most illuminating, but is not exceptional with regard to this situation. In other contexts this conflict is often represented as the rift between "Red" and "Expert." The Party and the managers could tend to find themselves at odds. Yet, as the system functions, such a portrayal is oversimplified. The debate turns on whether ideology is a means or an end. In substance, the alternative directions of Marxism are conceptualized: "Command" versus "Market" economy and general "centralization" versus "decentralization." At certain periods in the short history of socialist Yugoslavia this juxtaposition has been put in terms of "bureaucrats" versus "socialists." For at least some critical groups and levels in the system, the chosen path is clear. For them, ideology is not an adequate guide to meet the challenges which their routine responsibilities broach. In this vein, the enterprise elite is one clearly committed elite segment. To the extent that this investigation has examined "core" groups in the Yugoslav system, the proposition could be offered that the direction away from rigid ideological prescriptions is in evidence throughout the system.

Proposition 3. Decentralization in the many forms of Yugoslav self-management has produced initial signs that it is economically and politically feasible. One might wish to argue that this is particularly true for the stage of development in which Eastern European states find themselves in the 1970s. The record reveals that the new system is adequately productive and efficient, and meets the minimal criteria for popularity which supports the continued growth of the system and which to date has absorbed the incumbent social and economic dislocation, inflation notwithstanding.

Proposition 4. The policy of expanded symbolic and active participation at all levels of the system is adequately tempered by systemic constraints to render political and economic management sufficient power and authority to effectively lead, initiate, and execute policy. The Reforms clearly challenged and continue to challenge the political leadership to find that degree of decentralization which brings the desired ends without sacrificing the measure of control and executive (that is, centralized) authority to continue to effectively guide a developing country with all its traditional propensities and incumbent weaknesses. That point is delicate to establish and demanding to maintain. Annually we note systemic adjustments to external developments or evolving circumstances which threaten (in the perception of the political leadership) the balance.

Proposition 5. "Politics" and political components in the system, reshaped by the Reforms of the 1960s, no longer hold effective, exclusive control over the qualitative direction of change in the system. The Party and segments of the government continue to control the pace of change and provide parameters to the nature of change. System maintenance is perceived by the elite as a function of popularization and, as such, control mechanisms are low profile and indirect by design. Basically, the ability and propensity of the political authorities to impose broad, central, coercive control have tangibly diminished.

Proposition 6. The political response to systemic "liberalization" is conservative and wary and is framed in terms of "protecting the public interest from the economic interests." This concept implies a sharp differentiation of the economic and the political which is unclear to most of the system's actors with the exception of the "national elite." In essence, at the lower levels the public interest and the economic interests are perceived as being in harmony—directly related phenomena. At the national level this concern seems to be a reflection of a potential political insecurity which could and does germinate in the contemporary problems of the state—conflicting nationalisms, imbalance of payments, inflation, and the impending leadership succession.

Proposition 7. "Development" and "participation" (two of the three avowed goals in Yugoslavia) when at odds, are carefully compromised, usually on the initiative of the economic elite. Such tensions are not infrequent, and this expanding role is one of the methods by which economic elites remain politically visible and important on the national and republic levels. From the perspective of the established political elite, it is a relatively painless way, in a political sense, to resolve a difficulty. This pattern of compromise sponsored informally by the economic men in the system is especially clear in relation to functional as opposed to theoretical goals and policy.

124

Proposition 8. Yugoslavia has moved dramatically to governmental reform and in doing so has established and strengthened a formal channel for the representation of economic interests. Though organizationally weak to date, the political potential of these segments of government is significant. Other linkages at the microlevel of the economy, between enterprises and political authorities, are numerous and complex (often personalized), but are real and effective. The economic chambers and their more responsible and creative activity are signs of this crystallizing development.

Proposition 9. In Yugoslavia as in most Communist states there exists an organizational "hang up" over the concepts of "agreement" and "unanimity." This emphasis and expectation of consensus in politics rather than conflict grows out of the Marxian concept of "harmony," and is antithetical to the increased ability of the system to respond to developmental needs and challenges. Reality has changed, and is changing, this expectation of consensus which means that the system's formal structure is increasingly out of synchronization with the demands put upon it. This has created legal and constitutional debate in recent years, particularly among the national economic elite followed by increasingly numerous legal and constitutional adjustments.

Proposition 10. Economic executives in the system are system-oriented and will professionally respond to other than direct financial rewards. These elites are one of the principal beneficiaries of the institutionalized "rotation" of political elites in the system. Apart from preventing the evolution of pockets of entrenched politicians, the principle serves to co-opt managers and economists to fill political roles. This political experience, while limited by the same principle, yields a general awareness of political processes among managers and creates an identification with the problems and prospects of the system. Integration of the political and economic sectors and a commitment to common goals have been emerging as benefits of this new provision.

Proposition 11. The similarity of developmental challenges in other Communist states, including the Soviet Union and China, make the model of the economic and political subsystems of Yugoslavia and the working relationship between the two a focus of attention and consideration. The Yugoslavs tend to underplay their impact on other Communist states. Yet in numerous Soviet experiments, in events surrounding the Czech reforms, in recent developments in Hungary, the image of Yugoslav experiences can be found.

This examination, reflecting the objective set out in Chapter 1, has sought to pursue the organizational and functional routines of the

Yugoslav system with particular emphasis on economic matters. A commitment was made to deal with these phenomena as they manifest themselves on the microlevel (Direktors, Enterprises, and Politics), as linkages (Interests of the Economic Sector and Policy-makers), and at the macrolevel (National Economic Programs and Foreign Economic Relations). This initial investigation has yielded numerous propositions of relatively narrow scope as well as the eleven more general propositions. It discovered a fundamental change taking place among enterprise direktors and forms of economic management. It noted the increased authority and flexibility allocated in the enterprise and the maturing relationship between political organization and the firm in the local environment. Chapter 3 provided some insight into the pattern of interest articulation common in the economic sector. Gradual decentralization makes this feedback a subject of major significance. The economic chambers at the organizational center of this process have been experiencing the pains of adolescence in the system. The debate is set out, but the prognosis is only mildly positive. Organizational problems are particularly crucial to the final development of the chambers as an effective voice of this powerful sector. The Marxian apprehensions about the possibility of a socially responsible economic elite must also be mollified. Other factors, however, bode well for progressive change in Yugoslavia. The major renovation of the managerial elite in the mid-1960s, establishment of diverse purpose, nongovernmental economic organizations and consultative and financing corporations, reduction in unqualified ideological zeal, and a marked increase in the availability of both foreign and domestic economic literature attuned to the most modern knowledge on management practices—if perceived as contributing to a solid emphasis toward growth and development in the system, certainly all warrant guarded optimism. The Yugoslav record in recent international ventures of a business related nature is equally impressive though not without difficulties. The drift toward more developed and competitive markets is a sound indication of economic strength. Integration of the Yugoslav economy into the larger international economic community represents both a commitment of the central authorities in Belgrade (by its inclusion in the 1965 Reforms) and of the individual enterprises in the system whose interests, while specific—capital, machinery, technology, management, and so forth—are generally parallel to those of the system-at-large. These shared priorities are much more than a symbol of strength in the contemporary system. The Federal government in Yugoslavia has become the arbitor and coordinator of two principal inputs into the developmental process, the first, from the decentralized and pluralistic units (enterprises and republics), and the second, from the international environment. Balancing these forces over which the central government has chosen to exert only restrained or no control at all must stand as one of the fundamental decisions of the system in its history and as one of its greatest successes to this day.

This research has merely scratched the surface of the larger subject of the part played by economic elites in the expanse of social relationships in a socialist system. The project began with and now concludes with the notion that the degree to which direktors and top enterprise management have a primary role to play in the metamorphosis of the system has increased to proportions not generally recognized. The political implications, including reforms, organizational change, and functional relationships, are subjects warranting prompt and intensified social science research. It may be possible to learn much of the relationship between the economic and political realms in more established social systems by rigorously observing one that is in the early stages of development.

A recent issue of the Economist included this assessment of the Yugoslavs and their system.

> They do not lack admirers, either in the west or, more
> clandestinely, in the east, who applaud their efforts to
> try to create a combination of political and industrial
> democracy with an egalitarian framework. But the ruling
> hierarchies in Russia and China question the ideological
> validity of what the Yugoslavs are trying to do: their
> fear is that the Yugoslav experiment may succeed. The
> western powers, on the other hand, are worried about
> its viability: their fear is that this ambitious experi-
> ment, by "the best marxists we have got," as one west-
> ern anti-marxist commentator has put it, may fail.

BIBLIOGRAPHY

Ichak Adizes, <u>Industrial Democracy: Yugoslav Style</u>, Free Press, New York, 1971.

Rudolf Bicanic, "Economic Growth Under Centralized and Decentralized Planning: Yugoslavia - A Case Study," <u>Economic Development and Cultural Change</u>, Vol. 5, 1957, pp. 63-74.

Rudolf Bicanic, "Interaction of Macro- and Microeconomic Decisions in Yugoslavia, 1954-1957," in <u>Value and Plan</u>, ed. by Gregory Grossman, University of California Press, Berkeley, 1960.

Joseph T. Bombelles, "Planning and Economic Growth of Yugoslavia, 1947-1961," Hoover Institute Press, 1967.

M. J. Broeckmeyer (ed.), <u>Yugoslav Workers' Self-Management</u>, D. Reidel Publishing Company, Dordrecht, Holland, 1970.

S. Dapcevic-Kucar, "Decentralized Socialist Planning: Yugoslavia," in <u>Planning Economic Development</u>, ed. by E. Hagen, Irwin, Homewood, Illinois, 1963.

Jovan Djordjevic, "The Formation of Economic and Financial Policy: Yugoslavia," <u>International Social Science Bulletin</u>, Vol. 8, No. 2, 1956, pp. 287-298.

Jack C. Fisher, "The Yugoslav Commune," <u>World Politics</u>, Vol. 16, No. 3, 1964, pp. 418-441.

Wolfgang Friedmann, "Freedom and Planning in Yugoslavia's Economic System," <u>Slavic Studies</u>, Vol. 25, 1966, pp. 630-640.

George W. Hoffman, "Yugoslavia in Transition: Industrial Expansion and Resource Bases," <u>Economic Geography</u>, Vol. 32, No. 4, 1956, pp. 294-315.

Branko Horvat, <u>Towards a Theory of Planned Economy</u>, International Arts and Sciences Press, White Plains, 1969.

Branko Horvat, <u>Business Cycles in Yugoslavia</u>, International Arts and Sciences Press, White Plains, 1971.

Branko Horvat, An Essay on Yugoslav Society, International Arts and
Sciences Press, White Plains, 1967.

ILO, Workers' Management in Yugoslavia, International Labor Organization, Geneva, 1962.

Jiri Kolaja, Workers' Councils - The Yugoslav Experience, Praeger,
New York, 1965.

Georges Lasserre, L'Enterprise socialiste en Yougoslavie, Editions
de Minuit, Paris, 1964.

Gudrun Lehman, Stellung und Aufgaben der ökonomischen Einheiten
in den jugoslawischen Unternehmungen, Duncker und Humbolt,
Berlin, 1967.

William N. Loucks, "Workers' Self-Government in Yugoslav Industry,"
World Politics, Vol. 11, No. 1, 1958, pp. 68-82.

George Macesich, Yugoslavia: The Theory and Practice of Development Planning, University of Virginia Press, Charlottesville,
1964.

Stella Margold, "Yugoslavia's New Economic Reforms," American
Journal of Economics and Sociology, Vol. 26, No. 3, 1967, pp.
427-433.

Dieter Meier, Leitung, Besteuerung und Finanzierung der jugoslawischen
Industrieunternehmungen im Vergleich mit deutschen Aktienge-
sellschaften (Series "Sudosteuropa-Studien"), Sudosteuropa-
Verlagsgesellschaft, Munchen, 1968.

Viktor Meier, Das neue jugoslawische Wirtschaftssystem, Poly-
graphischez Verlag, Zurich, 1956.

Deborah D. Milenkovitch, Plan and Market in Yugoslav Economic
Thought, Yale University Press, New Haven, 1971.

Egon Neuberger, "Centralization vs. Decentralization: The Case of
Yugoslav Banking," American Slavic and East European Review,
Vol. 18, No. 3, 1959, pp. 361-373.

OECD, Economic Surveys: Socialist Federal Republic of Yugoslavia,
Organization for Economic Cooperation and Development, Paris,
1967.

Svetozar Pejovich, The Market-Planned Economy of Yugoslavia, University of Minnesota Press, Minneapolis, 1966.

M. Samardzija, "The Market and Social Planning in the Yugoslav Economy," Quarterly Review of Economics and Business, Vol. 7, No. 2, 1967, pp. 37-44.

Robert F. Severson, Jr., "The Yugoslav Economy: A Socialist Model," Dissertation Abstracts, Vol. 24, No. 12, 1964, University of Illinois, 1963.

Jozo Tomasevich, Peasants, Politics and Economic Change in Yugoslavia, Stanford University Press, Stanford, California, 1955.

David Tornquist, Look East, Look West: The Socialist Adventure in Yugoslavia, Macmillan, New York, 1966.

Jaroslav Vanek, "Yugoslav Economic Growth and Its Conditions," American Economic Review, Vol. 53, No. 2, 1963, pp. 555-561.

S. Venu, "Yugoslavia, 'Market Syndicalism' and Development From Below," International Review of History and Political Science, Vol. 1, No. 3, 1964, pp. 81-90.

Benjamin N. Ward, "The Firm in Illyria: Market Syndicalism," The American Economic Review, Vol. 48, 1958, pp. 566-589.

Benjamin N. Ward, "From Marx to Barone: Socialism and the Postwar Yugoslav Industrial Firm" unpublished doctoral dissertation, University of California, Berkeley, 1956.

Benjamin N. Ward, "Industrial Decentralization in Yugoslavia," California Slavic Studies, Vol. 2, 1963, pp. 169-187.

Benjamin N. Ward, "The Nationalized Firm in Yugoslavia," American Economic Review, Vol. 55, 1965, pp. 65-74.

Albert Waterston, Planning in Yugoslavia, Johns Hopkins Press, Baltimore, Md., 1962.

Igor Weitzmann, Das System der Einkommensverteilung in der sozialistischen Marktwirtschaft Jugoslawiens, Duncker und Humbolt, Berlin, 1958.

M. George Zaninovich, <u>The Development of Socialist Yugoslavia</u>
(Series "Integration and Community Building in Eastern Europe"),
Johns Hopkins Press, Baltimore, Md., 1968.

INDEX

agreement principle, 41, 48

Bertsch, G., 47
Blum, E., 63-64, 69
board of management. See
  Management Board.
business, and politics, 1-2, 80

Center for Industrial Organization
  and Development, 53-55
commissions, 43
communities, 55-60
community of interests, 55, 59
Community of Railways, 55, 57

direktor, 19-20, 66-70; relationship to workers, 26-31, 32

economics, and politics, 3-4
economic chambers, 8, 48
economic planning, 11-12; and
  politics, 14-15
economic reform, 13-14; and
  politics, 21-23
elites. See managerial elites.
Energoinvest, 63, 64, 65
enterprise, 7-8; party influences
  in, 23-25, 61-62, 67-68
Federal Chamber of Economy.
  See SPK.
Federal Institute of Prices, 46, 57
foreign investment. See joint
  investment.
foreign trade. See Yugoslavia,
  foreign economic relations.

Hadzic, M., 105

ideology, 70-78
Industrijsko-Poljoprivredni
  Kombinat (IPK), 61-63

International Investment Corpora-
  ration for Yugoslavia (IICY),
  52-53
Iron and Steel Federation, 57, 59

joint investment, 30-32
joint operation board (JOB), 31

Kardelj, E., 20

League of Communists of
  Yugoslavia (LCY), 11, 24, 25
legal codes, 10

Management Board, 40, 47
managerial elites, 19, 109;
  changes in the management
  elite, 65-66, 69-70
Mark, K., 72
Milenkovitch, D., 14

organizational development,
  51-61

pluralism, 5, 21
politics, and business, 1-2; 80;
  and economics, 2; and economic
  planning, 14; and economic
  reform, 21-22
private property. See socialist
  property.

Rankovic, A., 14
reforms. See economic reform.
rotation principle, 68
Rus, V., 26
Russell, B., 72

Savezne Privredni Komore
  (SPK), 35-43, 46-47, 49
self-government, communal, 8

Socialism. See ideology.
Socialist Alliance of Working
    People of Yugoslavia (SAWPY), 11
socialist property, 7
Spika, I., 61, 62-63
Sukijasovic, M., 31
Supek, R., 26

Veljkovic, L., 31

Wilkinson, D., 81-82
workers' council, 8, 22; decision-
    making responsibility and
    authority, 31
workers' self-management, 7, 74

Yugoslavia, capabilities,
    collective, 81-83; economic,
    78, 80; educational, 80-81;
    international, 83, 85;
    political, 81; economic
    system, 6-9; foreign
    economic relations, 104-105,
    108-116; foreign policy, 99-
    104; political system, 9-11;
    publishing, 85-93

Zaninovich, M. G., 47

RICHARD P. FARKAS is currently the chairman of the Department of Political Science at De Paul University. Previous to this appointment he was an Assistant Professor at the State University of New York at Geneseo. He has codirected the international project on the "Development of the Social Sciences in the Socialist Community" which culminated in a conference in 1973 at the Rockefeller Foundation's Conference and Study Center at the Villa Serbelloni.

Research drawn basically from seven visits to East Europe has produced contributions to Regional Integration: Theory and Research on Eastern Europe, The Foreign Policies of East Europe: Domestic and Foreign Determinants; the coediting of The Social Sciences in East Europe; as well as papers on developmental patterns, interest groups, change and policy experimentation, the nexus of politics and economics, and economic managers and their political behavior in contemporary Communist systems. His most recent project is the coauthorship of Communist State Systems: A Comparative Analysis, a forthcoming text from Free Press. Professor Farkas's research has been funded by the Rockefeller Foundation, the SUNY Research Foundation, the Education Foundation of the University of South Carolina, and the H. B. Earhart Foundation.

Professor Farkas holds a B. A. degree from Northwestern University and a Ph.D. in International Studies from the University of South Carolina.

CRISIS IN SOCIALIST PLANNING: Eastern
Europe and the USSR
                Jan Marczewski

OPINION-MAKING ELITES IN YUGOSLAVIA
                edited by Allen H. Barton,
                Bogdan Denitch, and
                Charles Kadushin

POLITICAL SOCIALIZATION IN EASTERN
EUROPE
                edited by Ivan Volgyes

THE POLITICS OF MODERNIZATION IN
EASTERN EUROPE: Testing the Soviet Model
                edited by Charles Gati

TECHNOLOGY IN COMECON: Acceleration of
Technological Progress through Economic
Planning and the Market
                J. Wilczynski

THE USES OF COMMUNICATION IN DECI-
SION-MAKING: A Comparative Study of
Yugoslavia and the U.S.
                Alex S. Edelstein